"*Vision and Prospects for World Peace* is a timely and topical essay that reminds us how some of the greatest challenges of the twentieth century—such as preventing genocide—are still very much on the world's agenda. Hoda Mahmoudi's analysis, although rooted in the tenets of the Bahá'í faith, also skillfully draws on a broad spectrum of scholarship and human experience to demonstrate how barriers to peace in the form of individual and institutional habits that lead to conflict can be removed. For those interested in the fraught question of how to create a more peaceful world, this is recommended reading."

   – Miles Bradbury, Professor of History and Co-editor of *Divisive Barbarity or Global Civilization: The Ethical Dimensions of Science, Art, Religion, and Politics.*

Vision and Prospects
for World Peace

Vision and Prospects for World Peace

Proceedings of the Inaugural Lecture by
Hoda Mahmoudi

Research Professor and third incumbent of the
Bahá'í Chair for World Peace
November 16, 2012

Additional remarks by
John Townshend
Kenneth Bowers
Dorothy Nelson
Suheil Bushrui

⌖

University of Maryland, College Park

VISION AND PROSPECTS FOR WORLD PEACE

© Copyright 2013 University of Maryland

ISBN-13: 978-0989917001
ISBN-10: 0989917002

JZ5534 .M345 2013

Suggested bibliographic citation for this publication:
  Mahmoudi, Hoda. *Vision and Prospects for World Peace*. Proceedings of the
  Inaugural Lecture given at the University of Maryland on 16 November 2012.
  College Park, MD: University of Maryland, 2013.

For more information on the Bahá'í Chair for World Peace, please visit:
  www.bahaichair.umd.edu

Publication production and editing by Michael Dravis, University of Maryland

Book interior and cover designed by Peggy Weickert, University of Maryland,
  Design Services

Cover photo designed by Lori Evelyn, LoriEvelyn.com

In grateful recognition of their steadfast support for the Bahá'í Chair for World Peace—and in honor of their visions for and shared commitment to building a more peaceful world—this publication is dedicated to John Townshend and Suheil Bushrui.

(From L to R) Professor Hoda Mahmoudi, Dean John Townshend, and Professor Suheil Bushrui. (Photo courtesy of UMD's College of Behavioral and Social Sciences)

SUMMARY

In this study, Hoda Mahmoudi addresses themes central to building a more peaceful world, including human nature and its capacity to mobilize for good and ill, the pace and scope of changes shaping global conditions, and the role of education in transforming not only individuals but also societies at large.

First presented in November 2012 as the Inaugural Lecture of the Bahá'í Chair for World Peace—an endowed academic program at the University of Maryland—*Vision and Prospects for World Peace* shares a concept of peace-building called a "worldview approach." "This approach," writes Professor Mahmoudi, "moves beyond nationalism and particularism and instead embraces a global, or 'globalizing,' view of peace that significantly expands and enriches the prevailing, Western-oriented model of peace education."

These Inaugural Lecture proceedings also include introductory statements by distinguished authorities on related topics such as the origins and history of the Bahá'í Chair for World Peace and the strategic mission of the University of Maryland, which focuses on innovation, entrepreneurship, and engagement with the world.

Vision and Prospects for World Peace contributes fresh perspectives to the vital and complex dialogue on the search for peace.

CONTENTS

ACKNOWLEDGEMENTS

This publication incorporates the proceedings of the Inaugural Lecture of the Bahá'í Chair for World Peace which convened at the University of Maryland (UMD) on November 16, 2012 under the auspices Dr. John Townshend, Dean of UMD's College of Behavioral and Social Sciences (BSOS). I would like to thank sincerely Dean Townshend for lending his distinguished patronage to the Inaugural Lecture, for serving as its master of ceremonies, and even more for his steadfast support of the Bahá'í Chair over the years.

The following individuals associated with the BSOS Dean's Office lent outstanding assistance to the Inaugural Lecture event: Julianna Bynoe, Sarah Goff-Tlemsani, Ann Holmes, Laura Ours, Deborah Rhebergen, and Nadine Dangerfield. Similarly, Jan Tunney did the same from her vantage point at the Bahá'í Chair for World Peace.

At the dinner that preceded the Inaugural Lecture and at the lecture itself, a group of talented UMD student-musicians provided beautiful musical preludes; these included Shirin Majidi, Laura Stayman, Sandy Wan, and Andrew Wang. Additionally, a group of "BSOS Ambassadors" (volunteer student assistants) helped ensure that the event ran smoothly: Leah Werner, Unyime Udofia, and Dan Lerner.

Laura Ours and Louis Maani (a friend of longstanding to the Bahá'í Chair for World Peace) kindly took photographs during the Inaugural Lecture, some of which are reproduced below.

Michael Dravis assisted with production of the published proceedings. He and Helia Ighani proofread the various texts that together compose this publication.

Finally, I would like to express my heartfelt thanks to my fellow speakers who lent prominence to the Inaugural Lecture proceedings: Dr. Wallace Loh, President of the University of

Maryland—who spoke at the pre-lecture dinner—Dean John Townshend, Mr. Kenneth Bowers, Judge Dorothy Nelson, and Professor Suheil Bushrui. Each shared wisdom and insights that will inspire and guide the work of the Bahá'í Chair for World Peace for years to come.

Hoda Mahmoudi
Bahá'í Chair for World Peace
University of Maryland
College Park, MD

Professor Hoda Mahmoudi and President Wallace Loh of the University of Maryland. (Photo courtesy of UMD's College of Behavioral and Social Sciences)

THE BAHÁ'Í CHAIR FOR WORLD PEACE
AT THE UNIVERSITY OF MARYLAND

The Bahá'í Chair for World Peace at the University of Maryland is an endowed academic program that advances interdisciplinary examination and discourse on global peace. While drawing certain initial insights from religion, the Bahá'í Chair's program aims to develop a sound scientific basis for knowledge and strategies that lead to the creation of a better world. Viewing humanity as a collective and organic whole, the Chair explores the role that social actors and structures play in removing obstacles and creating paths to peace. Central to this focus is creating a body of rigorously derived and tested knowledge that can be applied to foster the emergence of a just, secure, and sustainable international order, one that addresses the social, material, and spiritual progress of the global community.

Through an active program of research and publication, the Bahá'í Chair for World Peace collaborates with a wide range of scholars, researchers, and practitioners. Recognizing the value of a broad concept of peacemaking—which it calls a "worldview approach"—the Bahá'í Chair addresses the many underlying issues involved and employs perspectives from diverse cultures. In particular, the Chair is committed to forging international research partnerships that significantly expand and enrich the prevailing, Western-oriented model of peace education.

A core purpose of the Bahá'í Chair's teaching and outreach is to encourage students to cultivate critical thinking skills which lead to understandings about the complex nature of social change in the creation of a more peaceful world. Within this broad educational objective, students develop a set of values— including the importance of service to others—that are the basis of lifelong engagement in framing public policy in areas such as the social and behavioral sciences, science and technology, and the arts and humanities. Such values can also guide students in their international and civic life.

Chincoteague Hall on the campus of the University of Maryland, home of the Bahá'í Chair for World Peace. (Photo courtesy of UMD's College of Behavioral and Social Sciences)

The Bahá'í Chair was established in 1993 to study major issues of world peace as presented in *The Promise of World Peace*, a Statement by The Universal House of Justice (the governing authority of the Bahá'í international community). In acknowledgement of the centrality of this document to the Chair's origin and history, the full text of *The Promise of World Peace* is reprinted in Appendix 2.

Make a Gift

For information on how to make a gift to the Bahá'í Chair for World Peace, please see Appendix 3 on pages 85-86. For additional information about the Chair, please visit: www.bahaichair.umd.edu.

Dean John Townshend and Professor Hoda Mahmoudi outside the offices of the Bahá'í Chair for World Peace. (Photo courtesy of UMD's College of Behavioral and Social Sciences)

Editor's note: This publication reproduces the prepared versions of remarks delivered on November 16, 2012 at the University of Maryland during the Inaugural Lecture of Professor Hoda Mahmoudi as the third incumbent of the Bahá'í Chair for World Peace. The materials are presented here according to the original order in which they were delivered; they have been slightly edited, including some revision of words and phrases.

OPENING REMARKS

John Townshend

L adies and gentlemen, dear friends, honored guests; on behalf of the University of Maryland and the College of Behavioral and Social Sciences, I offer you a very warm welcome to the Inaugural Lecture of the third holder of the Bahá'í Chair for World Peace, Professor Hoda Mahmoudi.

John Townshend formally opens the Bahá'í Chair Inaugural Lecture proceedings. Joining him on stage are (L to R) Suheil Bushrui, Kenneth Bowers, and Hoda Mahmoudi. (Photo courtesy of L. Maani)

I'm Professor John Townshend, Dean of the College of Behavioral and Social Sciences.

I should like to begin by thanking the fine group of student musicians who have kindly and skillfully provided a suitable prelude to our proceedings. So please join with me in thanking them.

Also on the same theme, I should like to acknowledge a special group of students who are helping with tonight's event, namely the "BSOS Ambassadors." These volunteers assist with the planning, coordination, and execution of special events hosted by the College of Behavioral and Social Sciences. Let us thank them for their service, as well.

For the University of Maryland under the outstanding leadership of President Wallace Loh, and for the College which I have the privilege of directing, this is indeed an exciting time.

Above all, the Bahá'í Chair for World Peace promotes global dialogue and understanding, as do our College's other endowed chairs—the Sadat Chair for Peace and Development and the George and Lisa Zakhem Kahlil Gibran Chair for Values and Peace.

The existence of three endowed Peace Chairs underscores the over-arching mission of the College of Behavioral and Social Sciences: namely, to identify viable solutions to the world's greatest challenges. The faculty, staff, and students of the College act on this mission every day through our research, our partnerships, our teaching, our commitment to innovation and entrepreneurship, and our active engagement with the wider world.

Equally important, our College attempts to bring the wider world home to our campus by maintaining a remarkably diverse and rich group of departments, faculty, staff, students, alumni, and collaborators. We examine topics ranging from African-American Studies to Government and Politics to Geographical Sciences to world peace.

But even in our breadth and diversity we—as a college community—are unified in our desire to make a positive impact at the local, national, and global levels.

Regarding the role of the Bahá'í Chair for World Peace, every moment of transition—such as the installation of a new incumbent—is an opportunity to look forward and glimpse the lineaments of a yet to be constructed future. Shortly, Professor Mahmoudi will do just that by explaining the strategic vision that will guide the next cycle of the Bahá'í Chair's development.

Transitions also allow us to pause, glance back over our collective shoulder, and reflect on the nature of our journey and the pathways we have taken. In this regard, the distinguished speakers I will begin introducing momentarily belong to what can be called the "founding generation" of the Bahá'í Chair. Together, they embody the Chair's vital institutional history and living memory.

I should like to acknowledge very briefly one facet of that memory and history. Since the inauguration of the Bahá'í Chair for World Peace almost twenty years ago, the National Spiritual Assembly of the Bahá'ís of the United States has been a source of wise advice and counsel to the successive holders of the Chair, as well as to the University of Maryland's leadership.

The National Spiritual Assembly also has consistently provided the Bahá'í Chair with what can be called "the sinews of scholarship," namely generous financial support.

For these reasons and many more, I am deeply honored that members of the National Spiritual Assembly are present with us tonight; I would ask them please to stand and be acknowledged.

The University of Maryland and the College of Behavioral and Social Sciences are also very grateful that the Bahá'í community is represented here tonight by another contingent of its most distinguished members, namely the Board of Continental Counselors, who as a body are charged with assisting national Bahá'í communities in their development. As I ask them to stand, please join with me in thanking them for their service, as well.

Dean Townshend's Introduction of Mr. Kenneth Bowers

Our first distinguished speaker is Mr. Kenneth Bowers, who has served since 2007 as the Secretary of the National Spiritual Assembly of the Bahá'ís of the United States.

In recent years, he has also acted as the Assembly's liaison to the Advisory Board of the Bahá'í Chair. In that capacity, he has periodically visited the University of Maryland to participate in various Chair events and to lead strategic planning meetings of the Chair's Advisory Board.

Before becoming Secretary, Mr. Bowers served as the National Spiritual Assembly's Deputy Secretary and also published a well-respected study of the Bahá'i Faith. Please join me in welcoming Mr. Kenneth Bowers.

Editor's note: At this point in the proceedings, in acknowledgement of the work of the National Spiritual Assembly of the Bahá'is of the United States, Dean Townshend presented that body with the BSOS Dean's Distinguished Service Medal. When presenting the award, Dean Townshend stated: "This is thanks for your very substantive support, but more importantly it's for the inspiration and leadership you provided in support of peace and the scholarship so important to underpin its pursuit."

Mr. Bowers gratefully accepted this honor on behalf of the National Spiritual Assembly of the Bahá'is of the United States.

Kenneth Bowers displays the BSOS Dean's Distinguished Service Medal presented by John Townshend. (Photo courtesy of UMD's College of Behavioral and Social Sciences)

STATEMENT

Kenneth Bowers

I t has been said that civilization is the social expression
of the human spirit, that spirit being the aggregate of
our collective intellect, our culture, our values. In short,
those things we share and reflect together as human beings in
our common quest for good.

In our modern age we have become accustomed to the
idea that civilization progresses. But we are also keenly aware
that no progress happens on its own accord. The past century
has taught us that it is just as possible, and perhaps easier, for
societies to regress into destruction as it is for them to advance
along a positive path.

Bahá'u'lláh, the Founder of the Bahá'í Faith, taught that
human beings were created by God "to carry forward an ever-
advancing civilization," and that to do this requires unremitting
commitment to certain essentials. Together these describe the
means whereby every person can reach his or her full potential,
achieve lasting happiness, prosperity in its full sense, both
material and spiritual, and contribute a full share to society's
onward progress. These are described in *The Promise of World
Peace* [see Appendix 2], a statement from the Universal House
of Justice [the governing authority of the Bahá'í community]
that inspired the establishment of the Bahá'í Chair.

Among the essential principles upheld by Bahá'u'lláh are
the unfettered quest for truth, the commitment to education,
and the conscious pursuit of justice and opportunity for all.
Particularly, as we emerge into a truly global society, it is
essential that we cultivate an unshakeable consciousness of the
oneness of humanity, with all that it implies, including freedom
from prejudice, pursuit of diversity, equal opportunities for
women and men, consciousness of the organic interdependence
of all peoples on the planet, and the creation of a world-
embracing ethic that features international dialogue,

consultation, and solving our common problems with the interests of all parties sincerely upheld.

If humanity is to emerge successfully into the new world that is now coming into being, it will be to the degree that people of good will are able to work together to achieve these ends. The members of the Bahá'í community consider it a great blessing to have found at the University of Maryland partners who exemplify these very ideals.

This university has a demonstrated commitment to diversity. It has both an international vision and an outstanding record of community service here in the State of Maryland. It has above all a relentless drive for excellence in education. These values have proven themselves in very practical ways, for we ourselves have watched over the course of the past two decades as the University of Maryland has quite literally vaulted into the ranks of the most elite universities of the entire world.

In the case of the Bahá'í Chair, it was a member of this university's faculty, the late Professor Edward Azar, who had the vision to see the connection between the principles taught by Bahá'u'lláh and the values of this institution, and to understand the potential in such a partnership to advance discourse on peace and the means of achieving it.

We take great pride in the achievements of the Chair to date, and we wish to offer special thanks to John Grayzel, the most recent holder, and Suheil Bushrui, the original holder, for their outstanding contributions. Of course, we wish our friend Hoda Mahmoudi great success in building upon their work, and we are confident that the Chair will under her leadership reach new heights.

We also wish to offer a token of our gratitude to Dean John Townshend. We have come to know him as a man of principle and dedication, a true friend to humanity and advocate of the highest moral values.

Editor's note: At this point, on behalf of the National Spiritual Assembly of the Bahá'ís of the United States, Mr. Bowers presented Dean Townshend with a scroll inscribed with Chinese calligraphy.

John Townshend (R) receives a scroll inscribed with Chinese calligraphy from Kenneth Bowers (L). (Photo courtesy of L. Maani)

Also acting on behalf of the National Spiritual Assembly, Mr. Bowers gave the University of Maryland a check in the amount of $100,000 in support of the Bahá'í Chair for World Peace.

Dean Townshend's Introduction of Judge Dorothy Nelson

Judge Dorothy Nelson, as many of you know, is a leading figure in the history of the Bahá'í Chair for World Peace. Due to her numerous commitments, she was not able to travel from California to join us in person tonight. However, such is her attachment to, and affection for, the Chair—and the University of Maryland—that she has prepared a special video message.

Judge Nelson was appointed by President Jimmy Carter to the United States Court of Appeals, Ninth Circuit, in 1979. Today, she continues to serve the Ninth Circuit as a senior Federal Judge. She was the Founder and Chair of the Board of the Western Justice Center, which is dedicated to promoting peaceful resolution of conflict among children, in the Courts, and in the community at large.

Those of us in academia are particularly impressed by the fact that Judge Nelson holds honorary degrees from no less than seven different universities!

From what I know after several decades in university life—and from what I have been told by eye-witnesses—the establishment of the Bahá'í Chair for World Peace required overcoming more than a few hurdles, including financial.

In the early 1990s, when the proposal to create a Bahá'í Chair took shape and form, a Brains Trust was established to guide the process along, and Judge Nelson emerged as its leading figure. From the beginning, her steadfast commitment to the goal of realizing such a Peace Chair at this university was unwavering and ultimately, successful.

For nineteen years, from 1990 to 2009, Judge Nelson served as the liaison between the Bahá'í Chair and the National Spiritual Assembly of the Bahá'ís of the United States. In that capacity, she provided indispensable guidance and advice to the Bahá'í Chair that helped it flourish under what were, sometimes, extremely challenging circumstances.

The strong bonds that connect the Bahá'í community and the University of Maryland, most prominently embodied in the Bahá'í Chair, are in no small measure Judge Nelson's achievement and legacy. Let us now hear her reflections.

TEXT OF A VIDEO MESSAGE

Dorothy Nelson

I'm honored to be part of this very important occasion because I have a very personal relationship with the University of Maryland that I regard as my second home and with the Bahá'í Chair for World Peace. It was on January 26,1990, that as Chair of the National Spiritual Assembly of the United States, I met with representatives of the University of Maryland, College Park to sign a historic Memorandum of Understanding to establish the Bahá'í Chair. Chancellor William Kirwan, President at that time, and Dean Murray Polakoff, then Dean of the College of Behavioral and Social Sciences, among others, were instrumental in bringing this about. President Mote, Dean Irv Goldstein, Professor Edy Kaufman, Professor Jonathan Wilkenfeld, and Assistant Dean Cynthia Hale assisted greatly.

Judge Dorothy Nelson.

The origins of the Bahá'í Chair are rooted amidst the strife of war-torn Lebanon in the early 1980s. Professor Suheil Bushrui and Professor Edward Azar, then Director of the Center for International Development and Conflict Management and Professor of Government and Politics at the University of Maryland, were separately involved in working toward a resolution of the conflict devastating their homeland when they met for the first time in Lebanon in 1982. They found that a profound community of vision and purpose united them. When their paths crossed again in 1985, Professor Azar urged Professor Bushrui—who at the time was teaching at Oxford University—to come to the University of Maryland to work with him to realize their shared vision of world peace.

Also in 1985, the Universal House of Justice of the Bahá'í Faith released to the world its epoch-making Statement, *The Promise of World Peace*. Professor Azar was deeply moved by its contents and wrote to the Universal House of Justice on behalf of the University of Maryland proposing the establishment of the Bahá'í Chair for World Peace at the Center for International Development and Conflict Management.

Then, on January 22, 1993, in a ceremony attended by over 400 distinguished guests, Professor Suheil Bushrui was installed as the first incumbent of the Bahá'í Chair for World Peace at the University of Maryland. Professor Bushrui was and is an internationally recognized scholar in the fields of Anglo-Irish, English, and Arabic literature, including W.B. Yeats and Kahlil Gibran. He is also a specialist in comparative culture, religion, and interfaith dialogue.

It was my good fortune to be appointed by the Bahá'í National Assembly to be its liaison to the Chair. During my many years of travel to the University of Maryland in this capacity, I learned what it was like to be in the presence of a

A video message from Dorothy Nelson plays during the proceedings.
(Photo courtesy of UMD's College of Behavioral and Social Sciences)

great and gifted man who has been accurately described by his students and colleagues as "charismatic," "inspirational," and "extraordinary." Of the hundreds of letters written to him by his students, let me quote from just two: "Your class on the Spiritual Heritage of the Human Race was the single most influential class I have ever had the pleasure of being a student in. Please accept my gratitude for touching my life in such a beautiful way and changing the way I think and live." And also: "This course made me a better human being. I am glad to have taken a course that nurtured a part of me that has been neglected in much of my education."

Professor Bushrui's contributions to the cause of world peace are profound and significant. His commitment to the concept of the oneness of humanity and his belief in the emergence of a world civilization that transcends all racial, religious, and social barriers has contributed immeasurably to the discussion on values and the need for moral transformation and spiritual regeneration.

As I did not continue in my role as liaison to the Chair from the Bahá'í National Assembly, I cannot comment on the accomplishments of Professor John Grayzel, the second holder of the Bahá'í Chair. However, from what I have read, his contributions have been significant, especially in the international field.

The mission of the Bahá'í Chair is to develop alternatives to the violent resolution of conflict through conflict management, global education, international development, and spiritual awareness.

Knowing this, it was a great honor to be invited by Dean and Professor John Townshend to be a member of the search committee for the new Chair, a committee headed by Associate Dean Wayne McIntosh. It was an even greater honor to be part of a committee that selected Dr. Hoda Mahmoudi unanimously to be the third holder of the Bahá'í Chair.

I have known Dr. Mahmoudi for over three decades. She has a magnanimous and world-embracing spirit, a clear-headed approach to global problems, and an earnest commitment to addressing the problems of our times as a researcher and scholar. For the last ten years, she has served as head of the Research Department at the Bahá'í World Centre in Haifa, Israel. She has served colleges and universities in academic and administrative positions as a dean and a vice president. She has obtained many grants for her research and scholarly interests that are directly applicable to the goals of the Chair.

In sum, Dr. Mahmoudi is an inspirational leader dedicated to teaching, research, and scholarship that will extol values of peace and conflict management. She will be a champion of core values, and she possesses an entrepreneurial spirit. I extend warmest congratulations to the University of Maryland, to the Center for International Development and Conflict Management, and to Dr. Hoda Mahmoudi as the new incumbent of the Bahá'í Chair for World Peace.

Dean Townshend's Introduction of Professor Suheil Bushrui

Our next speaker requires no introduction, but I shall attempt one nevertheless!

Professor Suheil Bushrui is a distinguished author, poet, critic, translator, and recipient of numerous international awards. He is recognized worldwide as the leading authority on the life and works of the Lebanese-American writer and artist Kahlil Gibran.

Suheil Bushrui prepares to deliver his introductory remarks. (Photo courtesy of L. Maani)

Professor Emeritus Bushrui has been teaching at the university level for almost sixty years, a remarkable record by any standard. Currently, he is Professor and first incumbent of The George and Lisa Zakhem Kahlil Gibran Chair for Values and Peace at the University of Maryland.

Because he was the founding holder of the Bahá'í Chair for World Peace from 1993 through 2005, no understanding of the Bahá'í Chair for World Peace can be obtained without appreciating his central role in its creation and development.

During Professor Bushrui's tenure as the Bahá'í Chair, he placed special emphasis on exploring how shared values—which he defines as ageless principles like the duty to love our neighbors—serve as indispensable connectors bracing the frame of society on all levels: individual, community, national, and global.

Even before he came to the University of Maryland in the late 1980s, Professor Bushrui's work resonated at the highest levels of national life and international relations. Beginning in 1982, for example, he served as senior cultural adviser to the president of Lebanon. In that capacity, he was charged with helping to achieve reconciliation among the country's diverse confessional communities.

During that same period, Professor Bushrui advised the president of Lebanon in preparation for, and during, official visits to the United Nations as well as key bilateral diplomatic conferences, including at the White House.

More recently, Professor Bushrui has worked closely with His Royal Highness The Prince of Wales, especially on projects and publications related to the environment and interfaith dialogue.

In sum, if Bushrui's life and work are testaments to—and uplifting examples of—scholarship in action. Please welcome Professor Suheil Bushrui.

John Townshend (L) introduces Suheil Bushrui (R). (Photo courtesy of UMD's College of Behavioral and Social Sciences)

REMARKS

Suheil Bushrui

It is an honor to have been invited by our distinguished Dean John Townshend to introduce Professor Hoda Mahmoudi as the third incumbent of the Bahá'í Chair for World Peace. It would be remiss of me were I to omit, before all else, to thank President Wallace D. Loh of the University of Maryland for his wise leadership in promoting the best interests of our great institution and for his generous support of the Bahá'í Chair for World Peace.

It is with deep gratitude that we also remember tonight the late Professor Edward Azar, who originated the idea of establishing a Bahá'í Chair for World Peace within the Center for International Development and Conflict Management at this University. Nor should we overlook the sterling services and unique contributions of Judge Dorothy Nelson and her late husband, Judge Jim Nelson, in this connection: to both of them goes the credit for successfully establishing the Bahá'í Chair and guaranteeing its success. And finally, no words can ever express my deep admiration and gratitude to Dean Townshend for his inspiring leadership and support of the high ideals of education in general. To my successor Dr. John Grayzel, the second incumbent of the Bahá'í Chair, goes my heartfelt gratitude for the work he has done on behalf of the Bahá'í Chair and for the enormous support he has given me as the first incumbent of the George and Lisa Zakhem Kahlil Gibran Chair for Values and Peace.

෴

The coming together of such a distinguished assembly in support of Dr. Mahmoudi is so very important because I firmly believe that she will achieve excellence in her services to the University, to our American society, and to the wider international community. We are particularly inspired by the presence of our students, our faculty, friends of the Bahá'í Chair, and above all, by the gracious presence of the representatives of the Continental Board of Counselors and the distinguished members of the National Spiritual Assembly of the Bahá'ís of the United States.

Suheil Bushrui and Hoda Mahmoudi prior to the Inaugural Lecture. (Photo courtesy of L. Maani)

Dr. Hoda Mahmoudi comes to us with a distinguished academic career. She holds a B.A. in Psychology, an M.A. in Educational Psychology, and a Ph.D. in Sociology. Her academic experience has been rich and varied; she has served as Dean of the College of Arts and Sciences at Northeastern Illinois University, where she was also a faculty member in the Department of Sociology. She has also served as Vice President and Dean of Olivet College, where she was instrumental in an institutional transformation which won national recognition. Her innovative ideas of institutional change attracted the attention of various high profile forums, including Harvard University's Institute for Educational Management and the Wharton Institute for Research in Higher Education at the University of Pennsylvania.

Prior to joining the University of Maryland faculty, Professor Mahmoudi served as the head of the Research Department at the Bahá'í World Centre in Haifa, Israel from 2001 to 2012. In this capacity Professor Mahmoudi led with distinction the activities of the Research Department, under the guidance of the Universal House of Justice, the supreme governing body of the Bahá'í community. Her responsibilities in this context included administrative appointments and assignments at the national and international levels, in addition to the implementation of policies regarding research, translation, and textual verification of Bahá'í scriptures.

In an article published in 1996, a scholar of religion noted, "[t]he Bahá'í community has long honored learning. But," he continued, "it is also true that it has only begun, relatively recently, to cultivate the habit of objective scholarship about itself and its texts that is the modern counterpart of higher criticism."[1] In this regard, it should be remembered that no other religion has had its scriptural treasures translated into a universal language, as has the Bahá'í Faith, within so short a period of time. Those of us who have had the arduous experience of working on, transcribing, and analyzing sacred texts know exactly the unique qualifications of those engaged in such an endeavor. In this context, Dr. Mahmoudi's achievement during the last eleven years has been truly outstanding.

Upon assuming her duties as the third incumbent of the Bahá'í Chair for World Peace in July of this year, Professor Mahmoudi faced an immediate and urgent task, namely: redefining the core mission of the Bahá'í Chair in a way that balances honoring the Chair's traditions on the one hand, with offering new, innovative methodologies on the other. In this regard, Professor Mahmoudi's broad concept of peacemaking— which she calls a "worldview approach"—promises to succeed

---

[1] Miles Bradbury, "A Close Reading of 'The Most Holy Book,'" *One Country*, vol. 7 (January-March 1996) (available from [http://www.onecountry.org/oc74/oc7416as.html]; accessed 30 October 2012).

brilliantly. Under this approach, the wisdom and practical peace-building techniques of diverse cultures are valued and explored, as are the contributions and insights of both science and religion. There can be no doubt that over the coming months and years the worldview approach advocated by Professor Mahmoudi will help the Chair—and its community of supporters within and beyond the University of Maryland— transcend established peace studies and programs that too often are segmented into regional and functional specializations.

᠅

Our University has been in the forefront of educational institutions in promoting the principle of Unity in Diversity, which is a Bahá'í tenet and a cardinal foundation of what may be described as Bahá'í culture. President Loh himself has been the President par excellence in promoting multicultural understanding and a diversity that unites rather than divides. Our campus has always been a home where the Golden Rule, both in its spiritual and cultural senses, is respected and upheld.

This cultural diversity is embedded in the many institutions and programs that represent Hindu, Buddhist, Jewish, Christian, and Islamic cultures. And now the time has come to introduce into the University curriculum the study of Bahá'í culture, which can be defined, correctly, as a Culture of Peace.

The University of Maryland was ahead of its time when over twenty years ago it founded a Bahá'í-endowed Chair for World Peace. Now other universities are following suit and have begun to establish programs to study the Bahá'í peace message. For example, Stanford University Libraries announced that they have acquired a unique collection of Bahá'í books and manuscripts; a curator charged with assessing the gift stated that "the addition of this collection is a great foundation for a collection to provide resources for our researchers...."[2] Furthermore, the University announcement about the donated materials described the Bahá'í Faith as "the world's youngest monotheistic religion."[3] Similarly, UCLA is now drawing attention to its rich and extensive collection of Bahá'í materials, which will enormously help researchers understand major Bahá'í principles of peace, such as: the unity of religion, the oneness of mankind, the independent search for truth, the harmony of science and religion, the equality of men and women, the abolition of all forms of prejudice, and the need for a world commonwealth.

ﺟ

The Bahá'í Chair for World Peace at the University of Maryland is the first Bahá'í Chair established worldwide, and provides leadership in exploring the cultural dimensions of Bahá'í moral and spiritual ways of thinking and living. From its very beginning, the Chair has accepted this definition of culture offered by L.F. Brosnahan and J.W. Spencer:

> ...The word [culture] as it is used by the social anthropologists...refers to the total complex of modes of acting, of ways of thinking and of habits of speaking which are characteristic of a community; and to the products or results of those ways of thinking and acting, namely, the ideas, the beliefs, the conceptions of that community, and what the anthropologists call the institutions that they have built up – that is, the religions, the forms of government and administration, the agricultural system, the language and so on. In short, by the culture of a community we mean all the learned

---

[2] Cynthia Haven, "Stanford University Libraries Acquires Large Bahá'í Collection," *Stanford Report*, 6 November 2012 (available from [http://news.stanford.edu/news/2012/november/libraries-bahai-collection-110512.html]; accessed 10 November 2012).

[3] Ibid.

and shared activities of that community and the results of such activities.[4]

The leadership in this new field of research therefore remains with us at the University of Maryland and, truly, I can think of no one who is more committed than Professor Mahmoudi to the noble and vital effort to identify solutions to the world's greatest challenges that prolong conflict and prevent the establishment of peace. Under Dr. Mahmoudi's leadership, the Bahá'í Chair shall develop a sound scientific basis for knowledge—together with corresponding strategies—that will lead to the creation of a better world.

The major challenges facing the world today, and that demand the full attention of humanity, include the following: the threat of nuclear annihilation, the danger of overpopulation, the degradation of the global environment, the gap between the developing and the industrial worlds, the need for fundamental restructuring of educational systems, and the breakdown in public and private morality.

The agendas, plans and policies proposed by the worldly wise and defined by a materialistic approach are not by themselves capable of bringing about true and lasting peace. As Rushworth Kidder states in his book *An Agenda for the 21st Century*:

> Those policies are of uncertain value without the qualities of thought—the "habits of the heart", to use a phrase that sociologist Robert Bellah borrowed from Alexis de Tocqueville....[5]

In his last great work, *The Management of Protracted Social Conflict*, my late friend Ed Azar, who was the first to propose

---

[4] "Language and Culture," in L.F. Brosnahan and J.W. Spencer, *Language and Society*, four talks given for the Nigerian Broadcasting Corporation in February 1962 (Ibadan: Ibadan University Press, 1962), 9.

[5] Rushworth M. Kidder, ed., *An Agenda for the 21st Century* (Cambridge, MA: The MIT Press, 1987), 203.

the creation of a Bahá'í Chair at the University of Maryland, stressed the need for people involved in problem-solving forums to be "keenly aware of the ethical responsibilities associated with the process."[6] Shortly before his death, Professor Azar confided in me that his last book was in a sense only half written. We discussed the need for a book which dealt with the spiritual and cultural elements involved in conflict management—elements that we felt constituted a vitally important aspect of the whole issue.

This statement by the late Professor Azar was made twenty-two years ago. Dr. Mahmoudi, I am sure, will realize Ed Azar's hope and will create a program that will study the spiritual and cultural elements involved in conflict management and building peace. As Dr. Mahmoudi emphasizes, any peace program must necessarily deal with attitudes and values and highlight the importance of eliminating all forms of prejudice; but, more importantly, it is only when individuals resolve to pursue, as a matter of daily habit, the quest for self-knowledge, inner harmony and unity, that true and lasting peace will reign.

In many ways, Hoda Mahmoudi has followed the example set by her distinguished father, Dr. Jalil Mahmoudi, who was a prolific author, expert in agricultural economics, and Professor Emeritus of Sociology and Languages at the University of Utah. She has understood that in order to achieve the goal of world peace, it is imperative to propose policies that will help restructure education and, above all, encourage and develop universal education for both women and men.

Dr. Hoda Mahmoudi has spent, in fact, a major part of her professional life engaged in what could aptly be described as the "silence of good things." Her dedication, her commitment, her sacrifices, her indefatigable efforts, her sharp intelligence, her noble vision, and her capacity for winning the love and respect of others distinguish her as one of the great servants of

---

[6] Edward Azar, *The Management of Protracted Social Conflict: Theory and Cases* (Brookfield, VT: Gower Publishing Company, 1990), 122.

humanity and, in particular, as a promoter of the emancipation and empowerment of women throughout the world.

I came to know Dr. Hoda Mahmoudi in the 1980s. I met her first in the presence of her beloved parents, Jalil Mahmoudi and Badri Behnam, a remarkable couple who embodied the noblest qualities of human love and dignity. Her distinguished father was a poet, and her mother was his muse. Their love for each other was legendary, and they were to the last day of their lives a symbol of the Arab adage: "No relationship between two people is genuine and true / Until each to the other speaks as I instead of you."

The love of her parents and their loyalty to each other helped to create in Hoda Mahmoudi a sterling character and a nobility of mind and spirit, which are the most important qualities in a teacher, while character building is the purpose of all education. The atmosphere of learning and cultural refinement in her family provided what we see in her today: academic integrity and an outstanding capacity for harmony between reason and tolerance.

Professor John Grayzel, my successor and distinguished colleague, and I both attempted to establish, in the last twenty years, the foundation of the Bahá'í Chair for World Peace. Today is a very special day because we shall inaugurate the beginning of building, on that foundation, a magnificent edifice of peace, and our talented architect in this endeavor is our distinguished and honorable colleague, Dr. Hoda Mahmoudi.

Dean Townshend's Introduction of Professor Hoda Mahmoudi

Ladies and gentlemen, it is now my great privilege to introduce tonight's inaugural lecturer: the third incumbent of the Bahá'í Chair for World Peace, Professor Hoda Mahmoudi.

I began my remarks by emphasizing how the College of Behavioral and Social Sciences is devoted to identifying solutions to the world's greatest challenges.

Truly, I can think of no one who is more committed to this noble and vital effort than Professor Mahmoudi. Under her bold leadership, the Bahá'í Chair shall develop a sound scientific basis for knowledge—together with corresponding strategies—that will lead to the creation of a better world.

Professor Mahmoudi assumed her duties at the Bahá'í Chair in July of this year, following an extensive and lengthy search for a stellar candidate.

Before joining the University of Maryland faculty, Professor Mahmoudi served as the head of the Research Department at the Bahá'í World Centre in Haifa, Israel from 2001 to 2012.

Previously, Dr. Mahmoudi was Dean of the College of Arts and Sciences at Northeastern Illinois University, where she was also a faculty member in the Department of Sociology. Professor Mahmoudi served as Vice President and Dean of Olivet College, where she was instrumental in an institutional transformation that generated national recognition.

As an active scholar and researcher, Dr. Mahmoudi has secured and supervised significant institutional grants from prestigious organizations such as the National Endowment for the Humanities, the Kellogg Foundation, and the National Science Foundation.

I have no doubt that Professor Mahmoudi's wholehearted commitment to scholarship in action shall serve as an inspiration, not only to the students on our campus, but also to our entire University community.

Please give a very warm welcome to the third and current holder of the Bahá'í Chair for World Peace, Dr. Hoda Mahmoudi.

VISION AND PROSPECTS FOR WORLD PEACE
The Inaugural Lecture
Hoda Mahmoudi

"Memory is a protection against the risk of abstraction and political experimentation. It is also what enables successive generations to share the harshest aspects of the human condition."
– Thérèse Delpech, *Savage Century: Back to Barbarism.*

Hoda Mahmoudi delivers the Bahá'í Chair Inaugural Lecture.
(Photo courtesy of UMD's College of Behavioral and Social Sciences)

Dean Townshend, members of the Continental Board of Counselors, members of the National Spiritual Assembly of the Bahá'ís of the United States, faculty, students, my dear family, friends and guests visiting from near and far, thank you.

The University of Maryland under the expert leadership of President Wallace Loh continues to enhance its national and international stature as a leading institution of higher learning.

In President Loh's own words, "the University of Maryland is ascending." I am grateful for the opportunity to serve at this great institution.

Some months ago, it was explained to me that successive deans of the College of Behavioral and Social Sciences have been steadfast supporters of the Bahá'í Chair for World Peace. Although I am a new arrival on this campus, I can attest that Dean John Townshend not only continues but also enhances that welcome tradition. Under his able leadership, the College of Behavioral and Social Sciences has continued to rise by consolidating a worldwide reputation for excellence.

There is a senior University of Maryland official who is not present tonight, but he played an early and decisive part in the founding of the Bahá'í Chair. I am referring to Dr. William Kirwan, presently Chancellor of the University System of Maryland. In the early 1990s, when the Bahá'í Chair was struggling to emerge, Chancellor Kirwan served as President of the University of Maryland, and in that capacity he did everything possible to nurture the Bahá'í Chair for World Peace. Since that time, Chancellor Kirwan has remained a great friend of the Chair.

The Bahá'í Chair and its community of supporters owe a special debt of gratitude to Judge Dorothy Nelson and Mr. Kenneth Bowers, who both have served, successively, as liaison between the National Spiritual Assembly of the Bahá'ís of the United States and the Bahá'í Chair's Advisory Board. Over the years, both Judge Nelson and Mr. Bowers have provided wise guidance to the Chair and to the University of Maryland. Equally important, they have also helped ensure the financial security of the Chair.

As a new arrival at the Bahá'í Chair for World Peace and the University of Maryland, I would be remiss if I failed to mention the decisive contributions of my distinguished predecessors at the Chair, Professor Suheil Bushrui and Dr. John Grayzel.

Dr. Grayzel was the Bahá'í Chair Professor for more than five years, from 2006 to 2011. During his tenure, he built on the solid record of accomplishment that had already been achieved while further expanding the scope of the Chair's activities. Among the new directions in which Professor Grayzel took the Chair, he organized a campus-wide initiative called the "Semester on Peace" which created a pattern of cooperation among various groups and individuals working to build peace.

Finally, I must, of course, salute the person who guided the Bahá'í Chair from its formal inauguration in 1993 through 2005, Professor Suheil Bushrui. By means of his peerless scholarship, drive, and dedication, Professor Bushrui infused the Bahá'í Chair for World Peace with a unique vision that allowed it to make enduring contributions.

Among the numerous national and international awards Professor Bushrui received during his tenure with the Chair, I believe the one he may be most proud of was his receipt of the Juliet Hollister Award for Service to Interfaith Understanding. Given by the Temple of Understanding—a leading interfaith organization that works closely with the United Nations—the Juliet Hollister Award is granted in recognition of "exceptional service to interfaith understanding." Other recipients of this prestigious prize include the late Queen Noor of Jordan, former United Nations High Commissioner for Human Rights Mary Robinson, His Holiness the Dalai Lama, and President Nelson Mandela.

Ladies and Gentlemen, with your permission, I would now like to present my vision for the Bahá'í Chair and my assessment of its far-reaching potential. In doing so, I am ever mindful of my fellow Bahá'í sisters and brothers in Iran, who for more than 30 years have experienced social discrimination, official persecution, and untold oppression. Sadly, the campaign against the Bahá'ís of Iran extends to the field of education: young Iranian Bahá'ís are systematically denied access to universities. Tonight I am ever mindful of their sacrifices.

Introduction

The aspiration for achieving peace has been a central concern throughout human history. Generation after generation, men and women have longed for, struggled for, and perished for peace. In the twentieth century alone, it is estimated that some 60 million children, women, and men lost their lives as a result of war and genocide.[1] Even in this the twenty-first century, the human rights of more than three billion people, about one half of the world's population, are not protected.[2] The scholar Ulrich Beck has described some of the human rights violations that prevail today:

> Torture, genocide, ethnic cleansing, mass execution, abduction, political murder, violence against children, rape, human trafficking, slavery, illegal imprisonment, illegal treatment of refugees, exiles and immigrants, the death of handicapped people, violent theft, the trade in human organs, exploitation of prostitutes and…mass deaths caused by the vicious circle of poverty, hunger and sickness.[3]

The philosopher and policy analyst Thérèse Delpech expresses this view about the violent nature of our times:

> The ultimate consequence of modern experience—the annihilation of tens of millions of human beings in wars and revolutions—has already happened. The discovery of the means for the moral and physical annihilation

---

[1] For a discussion of genocide in the twentieth century, see Samantha Power, *A Problem from Hell: America and the Age of Genocide* (New York: Basic Books, 2002).

[2] Ulrich Beck, "War Is Peace: On Post-National War," *Security Dialogue* 36 (March 2005): 12.

[3] Ibid.

of the human race has already been made. It was not possible to bury the weapons that were developed or the moral barbarity that was explored in a desert where they would be concealed from the experience and consciousness of future generations. On the contrary, those extreme experiences have been globalized, often on our initiative, and weapons have proliferated along with the spread of knowledge and technology.[4]

Today every positive or negative change that takes place in the social, economic, or political realm regardless of its geographic location is felt throughout the world. The depth and breadth of the interconnectedness of the global order cannot be denied. However, the lack of ability and capacity of governmental and social institutions to accommodate the ongoing changes and in successfully addressing new problems is a serious threat to peace and stability. The world is getting smaller; the nations, more interdependent; yet inequality, suffering, fragmentation, and disorder are increasing.

In this situation, one is reminded of the Chinese proverb: "If we do not change our direction, we are likely to end up where we are headed."

The Bahá'í Chair for World Peace has a unique responsibility to advance an educational process that will create a body of tested knowledge that can be applied to foster the emergence of a more just, secure, and sustainable international order; an order that addresses the spiritual, social, and material progress of the global community.

More will be said about the Bahá'í Chair and its goals for advancing a new discourse on global peace. However, before doing so, I would like to take a few minutes to discuss two subjects that are central to any discussion about peace: the first

---

[4] Thérèse Delpech, *Savage Century: Back to Barbarism* (Washington, DC: Carnegie Endowment for International Peace, 2007), 23.

is human nature and the second are some significant changes that are reshaping our world.

Human Nature

Understanding human nature is essential to any discussion of peace because an examination of what scholars are learning about this subject highlights the issue of education and its potential for building a better world. Both the nineteenth-century doctrine that biology is destiny and the twentieth-century doctrine that the mind is a blank slate have been rejected as a consequence of knowledge that is being generated through research in the sciences of the mind, brain, genes, and evolution.[5] The psychologist Steven Pinker asserts that "nature vs. nurture are not mutually exclusive, that genes cannot cause behavior directly, and that the direction of causation can go both ways."[6] He explains that:

> Genes do not determine behavior like the roll of a player piano. Environmental interventions – from education and psychotherapy to historical changes in attitudes and political systems – can significantly affect human affairs.[7]

Today, unfortunately, aggression and conflict characterize our social order, an order that encompasses political, religious, economic, and cultural systems. In fact, many are resigned to the view that violence and warring are inborn human behaviors and, therefore, unchangeable. Such beliefs are often responsible for and lead to a paralysis of will among individuals, a cognitive numbness that is not easy to reverse, but which must be overcome. Here, the role of education is vital in removing unfounded views about human nature.

---

[5] See Steven Pinker, "Why Nature and Nurture Won't Go Away," *Daedalus* 133 (Fall 2004).

[6] Ibid., 7-8.

[7] Ibid., 10.

The historian Howard Zinn has challenged the view that human nature is instinctively aggressive and violent. In a 1991 speech he observed:

> There's a history of wars and a history of kindness. But it's like the newspapers and the historians. They dwell on wars and cruelty and the bestial things that people do to one another and they don't dwell a lot on the magnificent things that people do for one another in everyday life again and again. It seems to me it only takes a little bit of thought to realize that if wars came out of human nature, out of some spontaneous urge to kill, then why is it that governments have to go to such tremendous lengths to mobilize populations to go to war?[8]

Social and cognitive scientists continue to enhance our understandings of human nature, and some of their findings are worth pondering. In 1994, in a period of about three months, around 800,000 people—mostly ethnic Tutsi—were killed in the Rwanda genocide. In the aftermath of this appalling episode, the two sides of human nature—the good and bad— were exposed. We are already aware of the heinous acts that played out during the slaughter. However, little has been said about what we have since learned about the role of the so-called "rescuers." The term rescuers refers to those individuals who risked their own lives in order to save others, including the lives of those who were considered to be their "enemy." I would like to share examples of the types of acts performed by rescuers. An ethnic Hutu government soldier, despite the danger and threat to his life, saved the lives of many Tutsis by "guiding them through wooded areas during the darkness of night." A Hutu pastor sheltered and protected Tutsi women. And the

---

[8] Howard Zinn, "Power, History and Warfare," address delivered at the University of Wisconsin Madison on March 21, 1991 (Westfield, NJ: Open Magazine, 1991), 4.

mosques of Rwanda provided safe havens for members of all ethnic and religious communities.[9]

We have also learned about the positive side of human nature from the acts of humanity displayed by thousands of individuals who risked their lives to save others in the 1940s during the Holocaust. Holocaust survivor Elie Wiesel made the following observation about those who risked their lives to save Jews during World War II:

> In those times there was darkness everywhere. In heaven and on earth, all the gates of compassion seemed to have been closed. The killer killed and the Jews died and the outside world adopted an attitude either of complicity or of indifference. Only a few had the courage to care. These few men and women were vulnerable, afraid, helpless–what made them different from their fellow citizens?....Why were there so few?... Let us remember: What hurts the victim most is not the cruelty of the oppressor but the silence of the bystander.[10]

The discipline of Holocaust studies offers important findings about human nature. At the Yad Vashem Museum of Holocaust History in Jerusalem, what are called "The Righteous Among the Nations," referring to the rescuers who saved Jews, have been honored for their acts of valor. Their actions provide insights that help us to understand better human nature.

For example, we have learned that at first most of the rescuers were merely bystanders. They stood by as Jews were being persecuted, their rights restricted, and their property

---

[9] These examples are drawn from Paul Conway, "Righteous Hutus: Can Stories of Courageous Resuers Help in Rwanda's Reconciliation Process?" *International Journal of Sociology and Anthropology* 3 (July 2011): 218-19.

[10] Elie Wiesel, Foreword to *Courage To Care: Rescuers of Jews during the Holocaust*, eds. Carol Rittner and Sandra Meyers (New York: New York University Press, 1986), 2.

confiscated. But, after some interval there came a turning point, an intersection at which the bystanders decided to act; they no longer accepted the intensifying measures against the Jews.

Historian Wolfgang Benz explains that at the beginning it was the Jews who turned to non-Jews for help. When non-Jewish bystanders faced desperate Jews knocking at their doors, they were confronted with the need to make an instant decision. The decision to rescue the other is described as a natural human gesture, "taken on the spur of the moment and only then to be followed by a moral choice."[11] The rescuers are described as ordinary people, some of them acting out of ideological, religious or political principle and others without any such motivations. They were women and men of all ages, some were Christian, others Muslim, and some were agnostic. Among the rescuers were the educated, illiterate peasants, city dwellers, and farmers. They represented people from all walks of life including domestic servants, diplomats, policemen, fishermen, and so on.

Psychologist Ervin Staub's five decades of research has made him one of the foremost experts on the personal and social factors that encourage individuals to be altruistic. Staub's research has also examined the passivity of bystanders who ignore the needs of others. In his book entitled *The Psychology of Good and Evil: Why Children, Adults, and Groups Help and Harm Others*, Staub provides the following conclusion, which is based on extensive study:

> To briefly summarize, human beings have fundamental, shared needs. These include a need for security, for a positive identity, for a sense of effectiveness, for both positive connection to other people and autonomy, for a comprehension of reality. Another need, which emerges most strongly when the needs I have described

---

[11] See "About the Righteous," website of Yad Vashem ([http://www1. yadvashem.org/yv/en/righteous/about.asp]; accessed 1 November 2012).

are reasonably satisfied, is the need for transcendence. This is an aspect of spirituality—the need to go beyond one's own material concerns and beyond the self. When these needs are fulfilled, people are well on their way to harmonious, caring relationships with others, as well as continued growth in their lives.[12]

According to Staub, the passivity of bystanders "greatly contributes to the evolution of evil."[13] He points out that, "creating goodness requires active bystandership by individuals, organizations, communities, and nations. Speaking out can stop those who do harm from doing more harm, whether it is a child in a school, an adult in a workplace, or a group that is beginning to develop a destructive ideology."[14]

Given the evidence for the capacity of humans to "do good," I would like to share two additional observations. The first, as previously noted, centers on the fact that human beings are not instinctively prisoners of aggressive and violent behavior. Therefore, intervention through education and training can alter attitudes and change behaviors. Psychologist Jerome Kagan's research on cognitive and emotional development in children and moral emotions helps us to understand what he calls "the uniquely human in human nature."[15] Comparing humans to chimpanzees in relation to their attraction to new experiences, Kagan observes: "Chimpanzees seek new fruits to eat, new places to rest…but humans spend more time than any other animal looking for unfamiliar events that can be comprehended and new skills that can be mastered….The desire for and

---

[12] Ervin Staub, *The Psychology of Good and Evil: Why Children, Adults, and Groups Help and Harm Others* (New York: Cambridge University Press, 2003), 531-32.

[13] Ibid., 547.

[14] Ibid.

[15] Jerome Kagan, "The Uniquely Human in Human Nature," *Daedalus* 133 (Fall 2004).

the ability to adapt to novel conditions is due, in part, to the structure of the human brain."[16]

A second important observation about human nature is from the bioethicist Adriana Gini and the biopsychologist James Giordano, who state: "as evidenced by history, human beings are achievers…humans show a trend toward not merely surviving, but flourishing….human history is punctuated by our attempts to break the bonds of biological restrictions, and 'be more than we are'; our relative dependence has been overcome by forming sociocultural cooperatives, our fears appeased by myth and assuaged by knowledge, and our weakness(es) compensated by intellect and invention."[17]

Having reviewed what the latest research reveals about human nature, I would like to address my second theme. This concerns the monumental changes that are taking place in the world today which pose serious challenges to individuals, institutions, and our global society and which relate to the subject of peace. The scope of the changes impacts the entire planet and therefore requires solutions that address the globe as whole and humanity as a single organic unit. Above all, we must be aware that these changes bring both positives and negatives, both civilization and barbarity.

Changes Shaping Our World

Our global community is undergoing great transformations. Consequently, our conventional thinking about the political, economic, and cultural components of the social order is being tested on every side. In many ways, we have not kept up with the changes that are unfolding before us. Sociologists Ulrich Beck and Natan Sznaider, among others, have noted that the

---

[16] Ibid., 84.

[17] A. Gini and J. J. Giordano, "The Human Condition and Strivings to Flourish," in *Scientific and Philosophical Perspectives in Neuroethics*, eds. James J. Giordano and Bert Gordijn (New York: Cambridge University Press, 2010), 343-44.

social sciences are being challenged by these changes.[18] The same can be said of other scholarly disciplines.[19]

In light of this situation, scholars point to the need for a re-examination of the existing fundamental ideas and theories we use to describe "modern society." Beck and Sznaider, for example, state that "if the social sciences want to avoid becoming a museum of antiquated ideas,"[20] they must engage in a healthy re-examination of the changes at play in the world. In an effort to study realistically the pathways that may lead to peace, considerable attention must be devoted to adapting existing theories that are no longer capable of describing the changing world. By way of example, three trends can be highlighted. These are: modernity, globalization, and cosmopolitanism. All of these phenomena are indicators of the sea change that continues to shape the global order.

The sociologist Anthony Giddens has described modernity as another term for modern society or industrial civilization. Modernity lives in the future rather than the past.[21] As a dynamic force unparalleled in any previous type of social order, modernity is connected with "a certain set of attitudes towards the world, the idea of the 'world as an open transformation by human intervention.'" Modernity is comprised of complex

---

[18] See Ulrich Beck and Natan Sznaider, "Unpacking Cosmopolitanism for the Social Sciences: A Research Agenda," *The British Journal of Sociology* 61 (January 2010): 382-403.

[19] See, inter alia: Saskia Sassen, "Territory and Territoriality in the Global Economy," *International Sociology* (June 2000): 372-93; William T. Robinson, "Social Theory of Globalization: The Rise of a Transnational State," *Theory and Society* (April 2001): 157-200; Eric Nordlinger, *On the Autonomy of the Democratic State* (Cambridge, MA: Harvard University Press, 1981); Fred Block, *Revising State Theory* (Philadelphia: Temple University Press, 1987); Theda Skocpol, *States and Social Revolutions* (Cambridge: Cambridge University Press, 1985); Saskia Sassen, *A Sociology of Globalization* (New York: W. W. Norton and Company, 2007); and Diane Perrons, *Globalization and Social Change: People and Places in a Divided World* (London: Routledge, 2004).

[20] Beck and Sznaider, "Unpacking Cosmopolitanism," 386.

[21] Anthony Giddens and Christopher Pierson, *Conversations with Anthony Giddens: Making Sense of Modernity* (Stanford, CA: Stanford University Press, 1999), 94.

economic institutions, including a market economy and a variety of political institutions such as the nation-state and mass democracy.[22] As a process that is, or should be, open to change, modernity has now evolved from its origins as a Western phenomenon to what is presently called globalization.

Our second concept, globalization, is a widely used term described by some social scientists as the period that follows modernity. Certain authorities, therefore, refer to it as the "second modernity." Just as the emergence of industrial society caused a breakdown in agricultural society, globalization has transformed industrial society into broader social and economic relationships stretching worldwide. Globalization is composed of and creates social networks that can be located thousands of miles apart; yet globalization, through the communications revolution, has also brought about a "time-space compression." We no longer rely on a physical presence, but by means of technology can remove the limitations of space and time. As a result of such developments, we see a significant acceleration in the pace of life. Globalization links distant communities and expands the reach of power relations across regions and continents.

Globalization has its contradictions. For example, some scholars note that although the nation-state still has an important role to play, the world has moved beyond the old concepts of national and international. Sociologists Beck and Sznaider explain this change:

> National spaces have become denationalized, so that the national is no longer national, just as the international is no longer international. New realities are arising: a new mapping of space and time, new co-ordinates for the social and the political are emerging which have to be theoretically and empirically researched and elaborated.[23]

---

[22] Ibid.

[23] Beck and Sznaider, "Unpacking Cosmopolitanism," 386.

Another contradiction of globalization is that both the state and the states-system remain, but are subjected to major changes. Although the state has not and cannot disappear, according to the international relations scholar Ian Clark, globalization may be viewed as an "addition to, not a substitute for, the existing international order...globalization is not some process over and above the activities of states, but is instead an element within state transformation," or a globalized state.[24] Clark concludes that, "We need to face the seeming paradox that there can indeed be an international order of globalized states."[25] Similarly, the commentator Parag Khanna makes a distinction between globalization and geopolitics. He explains that "globalization involves free flows, especially of an economic nature, [but] geopolitics involves largely political and military efforts aimed at gaining control over, but frequently disrupting those flows...."[26]

The third concept we will consider is cosmopolitanism. Cosmopolitanism refers to a set of moral standards for living in a global order.[27] Kwame Anthony Appiah, a Professor of Philosophy and a member of the Center for Human Values at Princeton University, describes himself as a world citizen in this emerging global order in that he is a product of a mixed marriage. He explains that his mother was born in West England, and his father in the Ashanti region of Ghana. Appiah observes that today cosmopolitanism "is a temperament that is to be found on every continent...."[28] He defines cosmopolitanism as:

---

[24] Ian Clark, "Globalization and the Post-Cold War Order," in *The Globalization of World Politics: An Introduction to International Relations*, by John Baylis, Steve Smith, and Patricia Owens (New York: Oxford University Press, 2011), 554.

[25] Ibid., 555.

[26] Quoted in George Ritzer, *Globalization: The Essentials* (Malden, MA: Wiley-Blackwell, 2011), 114.

[27] See Kwame Appiah, *Cosmopolitanism: Ethics in a World of Strangers* (New York: W. W. Norton, 2006).

[28] Kwame Appiah, "Education for Global Citizenship," *Yearbook of the National Society for the Study of Education* 107 (April 2008): 98.

...the conjunction of two ideas. One, which it shares with a lot of people, which is some form of commitment to the universality of concern for all human beings. That's one part of it. But what is distinctive about cosmopolitan universalism is that it combines that sense that everybody matters, every human being is important, with the idea that people are entitled to live lives according to different ideals, different conceptions of what they're up to, what they think is worthwhile.[29]

Appiah continues, "So unlike many universalities, cosmopolitans aren't in the business of trying to persuade everybody to be like themselves. We like the fact that the world is full of different kinds of people."[30] However, Appiah is quick to point out that "where culture is bad for people...the cosmopolitan doesn't have to be tolerant of it. We don't need to treat genocide or human rights abuses as just another part of the quaint diversity of the species...."[31]

Decades ago, in her famous work *The Origins of Totalitarianism*, the political theorist Hannah Arendt offered the following observation about nationalism as a barrier to peace:

Politically speaking, tribal nationalism always insists that its own people is surrounded by "a world

[29] Whitney Johnson, "A Conversation with Kwame Appiah," *Mandala Journal*, 2009-2010 (available from [http://mandala.uga.edu/issues/8/appiah_conversation. php]; accessed 1 November 2012). Additional sources on cosmopolitanism include: Martha C. Nussbaum, "Patriotism and Cosmopolitanism," in *For Love of Country?*, ed. Joshua Cohen, 3-17 (Boston: Beacon Press, 2002); Lee Trepanier and Khalil M. Habib, eds., *Cosmopolitanism in the Age of Globalization: Citizens without States* (Lexington: The University Press of Kentucky, 2011); Georg Cavallar, *Imperfect Cosmopolis: Studies in the History of International Legal Theory and Cosmopolitan Ideas* (Cardiff: University of Wales Press, 2011); Magdalena Nowicka and Maria Rovisco, eds., *Cosmopolitanism in Practice* (Burlington, VT: Ashgate Publishing Company, 2009); and Roland Pierik and Wouter Werner, eds., *Cosmopolitanism in Context: Perspectives from International Law and Political Theory* (Cambridge: Cambridge University Press, 2010).
[30] Appiah, "Education for Global Citenship," 98.
[31] Ibid., 88.

of enemies," "one against all," that a fundamental difference exists between this people and all others. It claims its people to be unique, individual, incompatible with all others, and denies theoretically the very possibility of a common mankind long before it is used to destroy the humanity of man.[32]

Arendt's vision of a "common mankind," like cosmopolitanism's commitment to the universality of all human beings, points to the fact that the examination of humankind as a whole should be at the center of our theories and empirical studies, especially in relation to world peace. Knowledge must take us to new ways of conceptualizing the world as a unity. In this way, we can carry out research in pursuit of knowledge that is relevant and valid to our ever-changing global community. In this regard, Appiah places great importance on what he calls an education for global citizenship. He explains:

> Each person you know about and can affect is someone to whom you have responsibilities: to say this is just to affirm the very idea of morality. The challenge, then, is to take minds and hearts formed over the long millennia of living in local troops and equip them with ideas and institutions that will allow us to live together as the global tribe we have become. And that means shaping hearts and minds for our life together on this planet, beginning, of course, with the education of the young.[33]

The Bahá'í Chair: An Education for Global Peace

We have briefly sketched the barbarity that has formed much of our history, while also recalling the humanity that endures even amid the darkest moments. We have also explored the nature of the accelerated changes that chisel away at and reshape our planet into a future that, from early indications,

---

[32] Hannah Arendt, *The Origins of Totalitarianism* (New York: Meridian Books, 1962), 227.

[33] Appiah, "Education for Global Citizenship," 88.

is sure to be vastly different from what any of us can imagine today. Here, I would like to focus on the role of the Bahá'í Chair for World Peace, which is part of the mission conveyed earlier by Dean Townshend to "be a solution to the world's challenges."

In 1993, the Bahá'í Chair for World Peace was founded at this forward-thinking, leading university. The mission of the Chair as described in its founding document is "to initiate public forums for discussing the issues proposed in the Statement of the Universal House of Justice [the International Council of the Bahá'í Faith], entitled *The Promise of World Peace*."[34] The contents of the Statement provide the guiding charter for the work of the Bahá'í Chair. However, I would like to discuss the source from which these ideas originated. Over its history of almost 170 years, the Bahá'í Faith has taken an active part in raising humanity's consciousness on the vital question of world peace.

In December of 1919, 'Abdu'l-Bahá, who was then the appointed head of the Bahá'í Faith, received a communication from the Executive Committee of the "Central Organization for a Durable Peace" at The Hague.[35] Representatives from nine European nations and the United States had formed this organization, and its deliberations resulted in a policy statement that expressed a "willingness to accept military sanctions against countries that started hostilities without first making a good faith effort to resolve a dispute by submitting to international arbitration or making some other appeal to the

---

[34] See "Memorandum of Understanding for the Establishment of the Bahá'í Chair for World Peace," n.d. (signed by members of the National Spiritual Assembly of the Bahá'ís of the United States and representatives of the University of Maryland).

[35] Shoghi Effendi, *God Passes By* (Wilmette, IL: U.S. Bahá'í Publishing Trust, 1979), 307.

[36] Swarthmore College Peace Collection, "Central Organization for a Durable Peace [Organisation Central pour une Paix Durable] Collected Records, 1914-1919" (available from [http://www.swarthmore.edu/library/peace/CDGB/ centralorganisation.htm]; accessed 1 November 2012).

existing peace machinery."[36] The committee met throughout World War I to discuss the basis of a durable peace and it disbanded after the Treaty of Versailles was enacted in 1919.

Unable to visit The Hague in person, 'Abdu'l-Bahá instead wrote a letter of reply to the organization, which he dispatched by a special delegation. He praised the efforts of the organizing committee and wrote the following about world peace:

> There is not one soul whose conscience does not testify that in this day there is no more important matter in the world than that of universal peace....But the wise souls who are aware of the essential relationships emanating from the realities of things consider that one single matter cannot, by itself, influence the human reality as it ought and should....[37]

'Abdu'l-Bahá then expounded on the need for a comprehensive framework for peace, one that takes into consideration the many issues that negatively impact humanity's progress and one founded on positive values. In his letter, 'Abdu'l-Bahá sketched a plan of action that would support and advance the goal of world peace; this emphasized the importance of applying spiritual values while exploring solutions to the social ills which prevent the realization of peace. The principles and concerns set forth in 'Abdu'l-Bahá's letter, as well as the themes found in *The Promise of World Peace*, find their roots in the original texts written by Bahá'u'lláh, the Prophet-founder of the Bahá'í Faith.

In the late 1860s, Bahá'u'lláh, 'Abdu'l-Bahá's father, wrote to rulers and leaders throughout the world (including the Sultan of the Ottoman Empire, various European kings, rulers of America, the Shah of Iran under the Qajar Dynasty, and the Pope and other religious leaders) calling on them to gather together in their role as leaders and resolve their differences

---

[37] 'Abdu'l-Bahá, *Selections from the Writings of 'Abdu'l-Bahá* (Wilmette, IL: Bahá'í Publishing Trust, 2000), 311.

in order that their citizens might live under wise and just government.[38] Emphasizing the changes that were reshaping the world, Bahá'u'lláh described humanity as having reached the condition where it would have to be considered as a single common community. He called upon the national leaders to resolve their differences and find solutions to oppression and injustice. He reminded them of the changes that were taking form in the world which had, for the first time in human history, created the oneness of humanity, a condition that required cooperation among the nations of the world in resolving differences, removing inequality, and upholding justice.

Bahá'u'lláh asked the leaders to adopt a system of collective security based on a shared commitment to prevent, or respond by putting an end to, the aggression perpetrated by any one nation. He stressed the need to create an international, democratically elected body representing all the nations of the world in order to manage conflicts that arise between states. He stated that an international auxiliary language would serve as a mechanism for promoting world unity in that it would greatly enhance communication and consultation. Bahá'u'lláh went beyond the global dimension of change, stressing the need for the development of values at the personal level, which he said constitute the bedrock of society because they relate to the moral and spiritual foundation of the social order. He denounced oppression and corruption, stressed the necessity of trustworthiness and justice, emphasized the need for universal education to include values that transcend all cultures, and said that science and religion must agree.[39]

Vision for the Bahá'í Chair for World Peace

With this brief background, I now come to the vision and prospects for the Bahá'í Chair for World Peace. Situated at the

---

[38] See Bahá'u'lláh, *The Summons of the Lord of Hosts* (Haifa, Israel: Bahá'í World Centre, 2002).

[39] See Bahá'u'lláh, *Gleanings from the Writings of Bahá'u'lláh* (Wilmette, IL: Bahá'í Publishing Trust, 1990).

University of Maryland, where the key features of its strategic mission are innovation, entrepreneurship, and engagement with the world, the Bahá'í Chair's central aim is to create a learning community where students examine the complexity that surrounds the vast and complex topic of peace. Learning takes place through a process-oriented, dialogic, and reflective inquiry whereby the study of a body of knowledge results in practical means for the betterment of the human condition. Here the relationship between science and religion is central to the pursuit of knowledge and its positive application. In this context of knowledge seeking and application, the agreement between science and religion is paramount.[40] I say this because from a Bahá'í perspective on peace, as noted in Bahá'í texts: "It is impossible for religion to be contrary to science"[41] because both "constitute the dual knowledge system...."[42] Although science can offer methods and tools of inquiry and learning, it alone cannot define the direction toward which society should move; rather, moral and spiritual principles must face the scrutiny of science, and vice versa.

Viewing peace as far more than simply the elimination of war or the prohibition of the weapons and methods of war, the Bahá'í Chair draws insights from universal values, which are the foundation for an education for peace. Equally important to this foundation is the study and development of a sound scientific basis of knowledge drawn from any and all fields of study that can advance a more peaceful world and greater happiness for humankind.

In this context, the study of world peace is more than the elimination war and violence—which are currently the dominant means for managing international conflicts.

---

[40] See the following source (also reprinted in Appendix 2): The Universal House of Justice, *The Promise of World Peace* (Wilmette, IL: Bahá'í Publishing Trust, 1985), 18-19.

[41] 'Abdu'l-Bahá, *Paris Talks* (London: Bahá'í Publishing Trust, 1972), 145.

[42] Bahá'í World Centre, *One Common Faith* (Haifa, Israel: Bahá'í World Centre, 2005), 33.

Prohibiting weapons of mass destruction, although an important goal, will not move us closer to peace. Rather, peace stems from an inner state, one that is supported by values. Here, the aspiration for peace is an attitude, a will, and a yearning which promotes the discovery and implementation of practical measures for peace. The Bahá'í Chair offers a comprehensive framework for working toward peace. What do I mean by this? There are major global social issues which, if not addressed first, will continue to serve as barriers to peace. Although by no means an exhaustive list, a few of these issues are: rising global inequality, discrimination and violence against women, tensions and divisions caused by religious conflicts, a growing culture of hate, the scourge of prejudice and racism, lack of universal education, and failure to teach a concept of world citizenship.

To address these and many other obstacles to peace, the Bahá'í Chair will draw upon a set of values that can help solve social problems. Students study, discuss, and reflect on correlating values with the wealth of sound knowledge that is generated in every field of study. Similarly, values will be examined and their application explored in the search for solutions to social problems. In short, the Chair's goal is to utilize the strength that an interdisciplinary and multidisciplinary program for the study of world peace can offer.

I would like to share the following example of the kind of multidisciplinary approach the Chair will take. An advertisement for a program called Human Dimensions of Global Change reads: "The Department of Earth and Environment is looking for a candidate trained in political ecology, development studies, geography, sociology, [and] anthropology. The candidate is expected to utilize mixed methods to explore the impacts, adaptation and vulnerability associated with global change (e.g., natural disasters, food security, water resources, and livelihoods)."[43]

---

[43] Newsletter of the American Sociological Association's Section on Science, Knowledge & Technology.

Staying with the comprehensive framework for peace, the Bahá'í Chair will adopt what I call a "worldview approach." This approach moves beyond nationalism and particularism and instead embraces a global, or "globalizing," view of peace. Here, perspectives from diverse cultures are valued and evaluated. A network of scholars and international research partnerships will be formed representing multiple viewpoints on social problems. The worldview approach significantly expands and enriches the prevailing, Western model in the exploration of the possibility of peace. Viewing humanity as a collective and organic whole, the worldview approach will explore the role that social actors and structures play in removing obstacles to peace.

The worldview approach is all-embracing in its outlook, examining the disorders that impact all people and the entire globe. It considers the contributions from a diversity of peoples, cultures, nationalities, and perspectives. It blends and embodies the ideals of the East and the West, of North and South.

To further expand the reach of the worldview approach, the Bahá'í Chair, in recent discussions with Dean Townshend, has begun exploring steps toward the establishment of a "Global Council of Peace Chairs." The scope of the proposed Global Council will, in the first instance, bring together, in a spirit of collaboration, the three Peace Chairs of the College of Behavioral and Social Sciences. However, in due course, it will extend to other universities regionally, nationally, and especially worldwide. The Bahá'í Chair will assume a major leadership role in coordinating this initiative, which intends to enlarge the reach of the interdisciplinary examination and discourse on global peace.

The Bahá'í Chair for World Peace is committed to offering students a broad, realistic, and applied education for and about peace. Through a dialogic process of learning, the use of the mind, the expansion of knowledge, and insight into the realities and complexities of life, we begin to imagine a world in which we work toward applying individual skills and capacities in constructing a better world. This is a process of learning that is centered on applying values and knowledge toward positive ends that transcend specific fields of study and career paths. Regardless of his or her place in society, every student and individual can be empowered to embrace the transformative nature of the education for peace provided by the Bahá'í Chair.

The ultimate goal of the Chair's teaching and research is to explore new frontiers of learning about peace. The aim of this journey is pushing forward the horizon and exploring the possibilities before us. The astrophysicist Carl Sagan stated: "What distinguishes our species is thought. The cerebral cortex is a liberation….We are, each of us, largely responsible for what gets put into our brains, for what, as adults, we wind up caring for and knowing about."[44]

The Bahá'í Chair stands ready to do its part in advancing a new and innovative discourse on global peace. It will do so through diligent work, collaboration with scholars throughout the world, and research and publications; all intended to advance knowledge and understanding of how to develop a better world.

We are hopeful, confident, unafraid, and eager to labor on a creative path to world peace. Please join with us in this effort. Thank you.

Bibliography

'Abdu'l-Bahá. *Paris Talks*. London: Bahá'í Publishing Trust, 1972.

_____. *Selections from the Writings of 'Abdu'l-Bahá*. Wilmette, IL: Bahá'í Publishing Trust, 2000.

Appiah, Kwame. *Cosmopolitanism: Ethics in a World of Strangers*. New York: W. W. Norton, 2006.

---

[44] Carl Sagan, *Cosmos* (New York: Wings Books, 1995), 278.

_____. "Education for Global Citizenship." *Yearbook of the National Society for the Study of Education* 107 (April 2008): 83–99.

Arendt, Hannah. *The Origins of Totalitarianism*. New York: Meridian Books, 1962.

Bahá'í World Centre. *One Common Faith*. Haifa, Israel: Bahá'í World Centre, 2005.

Bahá'u'lláh. *Gleanings from the Writings of Bahá'u'lláh*. Wilmette, IL: Bahá'í Publishing Trust, 1990.

_____. *The Summons of the Lord of Hosts*. Haifa, Israel: Bahá'í World Centre, 2002.

Beck, Ulrich. "War Is Peace: On Post-National War." *Security Dialogue* 36 (March 2005): 5-26.

Beck, Ulrich, and Natan Sznaider. "Unpacking Cosmopolitanism for the Social Sciences: A Research Agenda." *The British Journal of Sociology* 61 (January 2010): 382-403.

Block, Fred. *Revising State Theory*. Philadelphia: Temple University Press, 1987.

Cavallar, Georg. *Imperfect Cosmopolis: Studies in the History of International Legal Theory and Cosmopolitan Ideas*. Cardiff: University of Wales Press, 2011.

Clark, Ian. "Globalization and the Post-Cold War Order." In *The Globalization of World Politics: An Introduction to International Relations*, by John Baylis, Steve Smith, and Patricia Owens, 544-58. New York: Oxford University Press, 2011.

Conway, Paul. "Righteous Hutus: Can Stories of Courageous Rescuers Help in Rwanda's Reconciliation Process?" *International Journal of Sociology and Anthropology* 3 (July 2011): 217-23.

Delpech, Thérèse. *Savage Century: Back to Barbarism.* Washington, DC: Carnegie Endowment for International Peace, 2007.

Giddens, Anthony and Christopher Pierson. *Conversations with Anthony Giddens: Making Sense of Modernity.* Stanford, CA: Stanford University Press, 1999.

Gini A. and J. J. Giordano. "The Human Condition and Strivings to Flourish." In *Scientific and Philosophical Perspectives in Neuroethics*, eds. James J. Giordano and Bert Gordijn, 343-54. New York: Cambridge University Press, 2010.

Kagan, Jerome. "The Uniquely Human in Human Nature." *Daedalus* 133 (Fall 2004): 77–88.

Nordlinger, Eric. *On the Autonomy of the Democratic State.* Cambridge, MA: Harvard University Press, 1981.

Nowicka, Magdalena, and Maria Rovisco, eds. *Cosmopolitanism in Practice.* Burlington, VT: Ashgate Publishing Company, 2009.

Nussbaum, Martha C. "Patriotism and Cosmopolitanism." In *For Love of Country?*, ed. Joshua Cohen, 3-17. Boston: Beacon Press, 2002.

Perrons, Diane. *Globalization and Social Change: People and Places in a Divided World.* London: Routledge, 2004.

Pierik, Roland, and Wouter Werner, eds. *Cosmopolitanism in Context: Perspectives from International Law and Political Theory.* Cambridge: Cambridge University Press, 2010.

Pinker, Steven. "Why Nature and Nurture Won't Go Away." *Daedalus* 133 (Fall 2004): 1-23.

Power, Samantha. *A Problem from Hell: America and the Age of Genocide.* New York: Basic Books, 2002.

Ritzer, George. *Globalization: The Essentials.* Malden, MA: Wiley-Blackwell, 2011.

Robinson, William T. "Social Theory of Globalization: The Rise of a Transnational State." *Theory and Society* (April 2001): 157-200.

Sagan, Carl. *Cosmos.* New York: Wings Books, 1995.

Sassen, Saskia. "Territory and Territoriality in the Global Economy." *International Sociology* (June 2000): 372-93.

_____. *A Sociology of Globalization.* New York: W. W. Norton and Company, 2007.

Shoghi Effendi. *God Passes By.* Wilmette, IL: U.S. Bahá'í Publishing Trust, 1979.

Skocpol, Theda. *States and Social Revolutions.* Cambridge: Cambridge University Press, 1985.

Staub, Ervin. *The Psychology of Good and Evil: Why Children, Adults, and Groups Help and Harm Others.* New York: Cambridge University Press, 2003.

Trepanier, Lee and Khalil M. Habib, eds. *Cosmopolitanism in the Age of Globalization: Citizens without States.* Lexington: The University Press of Kentucky, 2011.

The Universal House of Justice. *The Promise of World Peace.* Wilmette, IL: Bahá'í Publishing Trust, 1985.

Wiesel, Elie. Foreword to *Courage To Care: Rescuers of Jews during the Holocaust,* eds. Carol Rittner and Sandra Meyers. New York: New York University Press, 1986.

Zinn, Howard. "Power, History and Warfare." Address delivered at the University of Wisconsin Madison on March 21, 1991. Westfield, NJ: Open Magazine, 1991.

Dean Townshend's Concluding Remarks

Thank you, Professor Mahmoudi, for sharing the vision that will guide the work of Bahá'í Chair for World Peace in the coming years.

As we bring these proceedings to their conclusion, I am struck by how much the Bahá'í Chair has achieved, but also by how much more the Chair needs to accomplish in its work for world peace.

The generosity of the National Spiritual Assembly—as well as other donors—has brought the Chair to this point. Now, new sources of financial support are needed to sustain the Chair's ambitious "worldview" concept as well as new initiatives like the proposed "Global Council of Peace Chairs."

Those members of this distinguished audience who may be inclined to assist in the advancement of the Chair's vision should feel free to contact Professor Mahmoudi directly.

As a final note, I understand that the Bahá'í Chair plans to publish the proceedings of this event, so those should be available in due course in printed form.

Ladies and gentlemen, this concludes the formal phase of tonight's event, but I invite you to remain to enjoy the refreshments that are available at the back of the room and to continue our dialogue in a more informal fashion.

APPENDIX 1

BIOGRAPHY OF HODA MAHMOUDI

A scholar of international renown, Research Professor Hoda Mahmoudi holds the Bahá'í Chair for World Peace at the University of Maryland (UMD). The Chair is an endowed academic program that advances interdisciplinary examination and discourse on global peace. Professor Mahmoudi has served in this position since July 2012.

As the Bahá'í Chair Professor, Dr. Mahmoudi develops a sound scientific basis for knowledge and strategies that explore the role of social actors and structures in removing obstacles to peace and creating paths to a better world. In pursuit of this goal, she collaborates with a wide range of scholars, researchers, and practitioners. In particular, Professor Mahmoudi advocates a broad concept of peacemaking—which she refers to as a "worldview approach"—that draws insights from all cultures.

Before joining the University of Maryland faculty, Professor Mahmoudi served as the head of the Research Department at the Bahá'í World Centre in Haifa, Israel from 2001 to 2012. Her Bahá'í service also includes administrative appointments and assignments at the international and national levels.

Previously, Dr. Mahmoudi was Dean of the College of Arts & Sciences at Northeastern Illinois University, where she was also a faculty member in the Department of Sociology. Professor Mahmoudi served as Vice President and Dean of Olivet College, where she was instrumental in an institutional transformation that generated national recognition. She has presented her ideas on institutional change before various high-profile forums and participated in Harvard University's Institute for Educational Management and the Wharton Institute for Research on Higher Education at the University of Pennsylvania.

As an active scholar and researcher, Dr. Mahmoudi has secured and supervised significant institutional grants from prestigious organizations such as the National Endowment for the Humanities, the Kellogg Foundation, and the National Science Foundation. As the Bahá'í Chair Professor, she is committed to working with UMD faculty and students to develop innovative, interdisciplinary research proposals.

Currently, Professor Mahmoudi is writing a book about an American woman born in 1851 in upstate New York, who may have faded into Victorian obscurity had she not possessed an insatiable curiosity about the world and a strong desire to make an imprint of her own. When she walked onto the world stage she was already in her fifties, having just finished her medical degree and joined the Bahá'í Faith. In 1909, she responded, without hesitation, to a daring mission to work in Tehran, Iran, which would change the lives of thousands and reshape the future for women of her era. She established an active medical practice for women, founded an all-girls school, and engaged in educational activities aimed at advancing the status of women. Having lived in Iran for over thirty years until her death, her story reveals a remarkable life that heralded a global awakening. She spoke of peace in an age of violence, of justice in an age of inequality, and of progress in opposition to the forces of fundamentalism.

Professor Mahmoudi's writings on subjects such as formal organizations, medical sociology, cross national research, and women's studies have appeared in leading publications, including *Organizational Studies*, *Group and Organization Studies*, *International Review of Modern Sociology*, and *The Journal of Bahá'í Studies*. Her essay on "Altruism and Extensivity in the Bahá'í Religion" (co-authored with Wendy Heller) appears in the volume *Embracing the Other: Philosophical, Psychological, and Historical Perspectives on Altruism*.

Olivet College granted Professor Mahmoudi special recognition for her support of and service to students of color and for her work on diversity issues and international education. She is also the recipient of many awards and honors, including the Award for Excellence in Bahá'í Studies, the Hewlett Grant for Faculty Development, and the Professor of the Year award from Westminster College of Salt Lake City.

Dr. Mahmoudi holds a Ph.D. in Sociology, an M.A. in Educational Psychology, and a B.A. in Psychology from the University of Utah.

APPENDIX 2

THE PROMISE OF WORLD PEACE
The Universal House of Justice[1]
(October 1985)

To the Peoples of the World:

The Great Peace towards which people of good will throughout the centuries have inclined their hearts, of which seers and poets for countless generations have expressed their vision, and for which from age to age the sacred scriptures of mankind have constantly held the promise, is now at long last within the reach of the nations. For the first time in history it is possible for everyone to view the entire planet, with all its myriad diversified peoples, in one perspective. World peace is not only possible but inevitable. It is the next stage in the evolution of this planet—in the words of one great thinker, "the planetization of mankind."

Whether peace is to be reached only after unimaginable horrors precipitated by humanity's stubborn clinging to old patterns of behaviour, or is to be embraced now by an act of consultative will, is the choice before all who inhabit the earth. At this critical juncture when the intractable problems confronting nations have been fused into one common concern for the whole world, failure to stem the tide of conflict and disorder would be unconscionably irresponsible.

Among the favourable signs are the steadily growing strength of the steps towards world order taken initially near the beginning of this century in the creation of the League of Nations, succeeded by the more broadly based United Nations Organization; the achievement since the Second World War

---

[1] Editor's note: The governing authority of the Bahá'í community. The text reproduced below is from The Bahá'í Reference Library (available from [http://reference.bahai.org/en/t/uhj/]; accessed 30 November 2012).

of independence by the majority of all the nations on earth, indicating the completion of the process of nation building, and the involvement of these fledgling nations with older ones in matters of mutual concern; the consequent vast increase in co-operation among hitherto isolated and antagonistic peoples and groups in international undertakings in the scientific, educational, legal, economic and cultural fields; the rise in recent decades of an unprecedented number of international humanitarian organizations; the spread of women's and youth movements calling for an end to war; and the spontaneous spawning of widening networks of ordinary people seeking understanding through personal communication.

The scientific and technological advances occurring in this unusually blessed century portend a great surge forward in the social evolution of the planet, and indicate the means by which the practical problems of humanity may be solved. They provide, indeed, the very means for the administration of the complex life of a united world. Yet barriers persist. Doubts, misconceptions, prejudices, suspicions and narrow self-interest beset nations and peoples in their relations one to another.

It is out of a deep sense of spiritual and moral duty that we are impelled at this opportune moment to invite your attention to the penetrating insights first communicated to the rulers of mankind more than a century ago by Bahá'u'lláh, Founder of the Bahá'í Faith, of which we are the Trustees.

"The winds of despair," Bahá'u'lláh wrote, "are, alas, blowing from every direction, and the strife that divides and afflicts the human race is daily increasing. The signs of impending convulsions and chaos can now be discerned, inasmuch as the prevailing order appears to be lamentably defective." This prophetic judgement has been amply confirmed by the common experience of humanity. Flaws in the prevailing order are conspicuous in the inability of sovereign states organized as United Nations to exorcize the spectre of war, the threatened collapse of the international economic order, the spread of anarchy and terrorism, and the intense suffering which these and other afflictions are causing to increasing millions. Indeed, so much have aggression and conflict come to characterize our social, economic and religious systems, that many have succumbed to the view that such behaviour is intrinsic to human nature and therefore ineradicable.

With the entrenchment of this view, a paralyzing contradiction has developed in human affairs. On the one hand, people of all nations proclaim not only their readiness but their longing for peace and harmony, for an end to the harrowing apprehensions tormenting their daily lives. On the other, uncritical assent is given to the proposition that human beings are incorrigibly selfish and aggressive and thus incapable of erecting a social system at once progressive and peaceful, dynamic and harmonious, a system giving free play to individual creativity and initiative but based on co-operation and reciprocity.

As the need for peace becomes more urgent, this fundamental contradiction, which hinders its realization, demands a reassessment of the assumptions upon which the commonly held view of mankind's historical predicament is based. Dispassionately examined, the evidence reveals that such conduct, far from expressing man's true self, represents a distortion of the human spirit. Satisfaction on this point will enable all people to set in motion constructive social forces which, because they are consistent with human nature, will encourage harmony and co-operation instead of war and conflict.

To choose such a course is not to deny humanity's past but to understand it. The Bahá'í Faith regards the current world confusion and calamitous condition in human affairs as a natural phase in an organic process leading ultimately and irresistibly to the unification of the human race in a single social order whose boundaries are those of the planet. The human race, as a distinct, organic unit, has passed through evolutionary stages analogous to the stages of infancy and childhood in the lives of its individual members, and is now in the culminating period of its turbulent adolescence approaching its long-awaited coming of age.

A candid acknowledgement that prejudice, war and exploitation have been the expression of immature stages in a vast historical process and that the human race is today experiencing the unavoidable tumult which marks its collective coming of age is not a reason for despair but a prerequisite to undertaking the stupendous enterprise of building a peaceful world. That such an enterprise is possible, that the necessary constructive forces do exist, that unifying social structures can be erected, is the theme we urge you to examine.

Whatever suffering and turmoil the years immediately ahead may hold, however dark the immediate circumstances, the Bahá'í community believes that humanity can confront this supreme trial with confidence in its ultimate outcome. Far from signalizing the end of civilization, the convulsive changes towards which humanity is being ever more rapidly impelled will serve to release the "potentialities inherent in the station of man" and reveal "the full measure of his destiny on earth, the innate excellence of his reality."

I

The endowments which distinguish the human race from all other forms of life are summed up in what is known as the human spirit; the mind is its essential quality. These endowments have enabled humanity to build civilizations and to prosper materially. But such accomplishments alone have never satisfied the human spirit, whose mysterious nature inclines it towards transcendence, a reaching towards an invisible realm, towards the ultimate reality, that unknowable essence of essences called God. The religions brought to mankind by a succession of spiritual luminaries have been the primary link between humanity and that ultimate reality, and have galvanized and refined mankind's capacity to achieve spiritual success together with social progress.

No serious attempt to set human affairs aright, to achieve world peace, can ignore religion. Man's perception and practice of it are largely the stuff of history. An eminent historian described religion as a "faculty of human nature." That the perversion of this faculty has contributed to much of the confusion in society and the conflicts in and between individuals can hardly be denied. But neither can any fair-minded observer discount the preponderating influence exerted by religion on the vital expressions of civilization. Furthermore, its indispensability to social order has repeatedly been demonstrated by its direct effect on laws and morality.

Writing of religion as a social force, Bahá'u'lláh said: "Religion is the greatest of all means for the establishment of order in the world and for the peaceful contentment of all that dwell therein." Referring to the eclipse or corruption of religion, he wrote: "Should the lamp of religion be obscured, chaos and confusion will ensue, and the lights of fairness, of justice, of tranquillity and peace cease to shine." In an enumeration of such consequences the Bahá'í writings point out that the "perversion of human nature, the degradation of human conduct, the corruption and dissolution of human institutions, reveal themselves, under such circumstances, in their worst and most revolting aspects. Human character is debased, confidence is shaken, the nerves of discipline are relaxed, the voice of human conscience is stilled, the sense of decency and shame is obscured, conceptions of duty, of solidarity, of reciprocity and loyalty are distorted, and the very feeling of peacefulness, of joy and of hope is gradually extinguished."

If, therefore, humanity has come to a point of paralyzing conflict it must look to itself, to its own negligence, to the siren voices to which it has listened, for the source of the misunderstandings and confusion perpetrated in the name of religion. Those who have held blindly and selfishly to their particular orthodoxies, who have imposed on their votaries erroneous and conflicting interpretations of the pronouncements of the Prophets of God, bear heavy responsibility for this confusion—a confusion compounded by the artificial barriers erected between faith and reason, science and religion. For from a fair-minded examination of the actual utterances of the Founders of the great religions, and of the social milieus in which they were obliged to carry out their missions, there is nothing to support the contentions and prejudices deranging the religious communities of mankind and therefore all human affairs.

The teaching that we should treat others as we ourselves would wish to be treated, an ethic variously repeated in all the great religions, lends force to this latter observation in two particular respects: it sums up the moral attitude, the peace-inducing aspect, extending through these religions irrespective of their place or time of origin; it also signifies an aspect of unity which is their essential virtue, a virtue mankind in its disjointed view of history has failed to appreciate.

Had humanity seen the Educators of its collective childhood in their true character, as agents of one civilizing process, it would no doubt have reaped incalculably greater benefits from the cumulative effects of their successive missions. This, alas, it failed to do.

The resurgence of fanatical religious fervour occurring in many lands cannot be regarded as more than a dying convulsion. The very nature of the violent and disruptive phenomena associated with it testifies to the spiritual bankruptcy it represents. Indeed, one of the strangest and saddest features of the current outbreak of religious fanaticism is the extent to which, in each case, it is undermining not only the spiritual values which are conducive to the unity of mankind but also those unique moral victories won by the particular religion it purports to serve.

However vital a force religion has been in the history of mankind, and however dramatic the current resurgence of militant religious fanaticism, religion and religious institutions have, for many decades, been viewed by increasing numbers of people as irrelevant to the major concerns of the modern world. In its place they have turned either to the hedonistic pursuit of material satisfactions or to the following of man-made ideologies designed to rescue society from the evident evils under which it groans. All too many of these ideologies, alas, instead of embracing the concept of the oneness of mankind and promoting the increase of concord among different peoples, have tended to deify the state, to subordinate the rest of mankind to one nation, race or class, to attempt to suppress all discussion and interchange of ideas, or to callously abandon starving millions to the operations of a market system that all too clearly is aggravating the plight of the majority of mankind, while enabling small sections to live in a condition of affluence scarcely dreamed of by our forebears.

How tragic is the record of the substitute faiths that the worldly-wise of our age have created. In the massive disillusionment of entire populations who have been taught to worship at their altars can be read history's irreversible verdict on their value. The fruits these doctrines have produced, after decades of an increasingly unrestrained exercise of power by those who owe their ascendancy in human affairs to them, are the social and economic ills that blight every region of our world in the closing years of the twentieth century. Underlying all these outward afflictions is the spiritual damage reflected in the apathy that has gripped the mass of the peoples of all nations and by the extinction of hope in the hearts of deprived and anguished millions.

The time has come when those who preach the dogmas of materialism, whether of the east or the west, whether of capitalism or socialism, must give account of the moral stewardship they have presumed to exercise. Where is the "new world" promised by these ideologies? Where is the international peace to whose ideals they proclaim their devotion? Where are the breakthroughs into new realms of cultural achievement produced by the aggrandizement of this race, of that nation or of a particular class? Why is the vast majority of the world's peoples sinking ever deeper into hunger and wretchedness when wealth on a scale undreamed of by the Pharaohs, the Caesars, or even the imperialist powers of the nineteenth century is at the disposal of the present arbiters of human affairs?

Most particularly, it is in the glorification of material pursuits, at once the progenitor and common feature of all such ideologies, that we find the roots which nourish the falsehood that human beings are incorrigibly selfish and aggressive. It is here that the ground must be cleared for the building of a new world fit for our descendants.

That materialistic ideals have, in the light of experience, failed to satisfy the needs of mankind calls for an honest acknowledgement that a fresh effort must now be made to find the solutions to the agonizing problems of the planet. The intolerable conditions pervading society bespeak a common failure of all, a circumstance which tends to incite rather than relieve the entrenchment on every side. Clearly, a common remedial effort is urgently required. It is primarily a matter of attitude. Will humanity continue in its waywardness, holding to outworn concepts and unworkable assumptions? Or will its leaders, regardless of ideology, step forth and, with a resolute will, consult together in a united search for appropriate solutions?

Those who care for the future of the human race may well ponder this advice. "If long-cherished ideals and time-honoured institutions, if certain social assumptions and religious formulae have ceased to promote the welfare of the generality of mankind, if they no longer minister to the needs of a continually evolving humanity, let them be swept away and relegated to the limbo of obsolescent and forgotten doctrines. Why should these, in a world subject to the immutable law of change and decay, be exempt from the deterioration that must needs overtake every human institution? For legal standards, political and economic theories are solely designed to safeguard the interests of humanity as a whole, and not humanity to be crucified for the preservation of the integrity of any particular law or doctrine."

II

Banning nuclear weapons, prohibiting the use of poison gases, or outlawing germ warfare will not remove the root causes of war. However important such practical measures obviously are as elements of the peace process, they are in themselves too superficial to exert enduring influence. Peoples are ingenious enough to invent yet other forms of warfare, and to use food, raw materials, finance, industrial power, ideology, and terrorism to subvert one another in an endless quest for supremacy and dominion. Nor can the present massive dislocation in the affairs of humanity be resolved through the settlement of specific conflicts or disagreements among nations. A genuine universal framework must be adopted.

Certainly, there is no lack of recognition by national leaders of the world-wide character of the problem, which is self-evident in the mounting issues that confront them daily. And there are the accumulating studies and solutions proposed by many concerned and enlightened groups as well as by agencies of the United Nations, to remove any possibility of ignorance as to the challenging requirements to be met. There is, however, a paralysis of will; and it is this that must be carefully examined and resolutely dealt with. This paralysis is rooted, as we have stated, in a deep-seated conviction of the inevitable quarrelsomeness of mankind, which has led to the reluctance to entertain the possibility of subordinating national self-interest to the requirements of world order, and in an unwillingness to face courageously the far-reaching implications of establishing a united world authority. It is also traceable to the incapacity of largely ignorant and subjugated masses to articulate their desire for a new order in which they can live in peace, harmony and prosperity with all humanity.

The tentative steps towards world order, especially since World War II, give hopeful signs. The increasing tendency of groups of nations to formalize relationships which enable them to co-operate in matters of mutual interest suggests that eventually all nations could overcome this paralysis. The Association of South East Asian Nations, the Caribbean Community and Common Market, the Central American Common Market, the Council for Mutual Economic Assistance, the European Communities, the League of Arab States, the Organization of African Unity, the Organization of American States, the South Pacific Forum—all the joint endeavours represented by such organizations prepare the path to world order.

The increasing attention being focused on some of the most deep-rooted problems of the planet is yet another hopeful sign. Despite the obvious shortcomings of the United Nations, the more than two score declarations and conventions adopted by that organization, even where governments have not been enthusiastic in their commitment, have given ordinary people a sense of a new lease on life. The Universal Declaration of Human Rights, the Convention on the Prevention and Punishment of the Crime of Genocide, and the similar measures concerned with eliminating all forms of discrimination based on race, sex or religious belief; upholding the rights of the child; protecting all persons against being subjected to torture; eradicating hunger and malnutrition; using scientific and technological progress in the interest of peace and the benefit of mankind—all such measures, if courageously enforced and expanded, will advance the day when the spectre of war will have lost its power to dominate international relations. There is no need to stress the significance of the issues addressed by these declarations and conventions. However, a few such issues, because of their immediate relevance to establishing world peace, deserve additional comment.

Racism, one of the most baneful and persistent evils, is a major barrier to peace. Its practice perpetrates too outrageous a violation of the dignity of human beings to be countenanced under any pretext. Racism retards the unfoldment of the boundless potentialities of its victims, corrupts its perpetrators, and blights human progress. Recognition of the oneness of mankind, implemented by appropriate legal measures, must be universally upheld if this problem is to be overcome.

The inordinate disparity between rich and poor, a source of acute suffering, keeps the world in a state of instability, virtually on the brink of war. Few societies have dealt effectively with this situation. The solution calls for the combined application of spiritual, moral and practical approaches. A fresh look at the problem is required, entailing consultation with experts from a wide spectrum of disciplines, devoid of economic and ideological polemics, and involving the people directly affected in the decisions that must urgently be made. It is an issue that is bound up not only with the necessity for eliminating extremes of wealth and poverty but also with those spiritual verities the understanding of which can produce a new universal attitude. Fostering such an attitude is itself a major part of the solution.

Unbridled nationalism, as distinguished from a sane and legitimate patriotism, must give way to a wider loyalty, to the love of humanity as a whole. Bahá'u'lláh's statement is: "The earth is but one country, and mankind its citizens." The concept of world citizenship is a direct result of the contraction of the world into a single neighbourhood through scientific advances and of the indisputable interdependence of nations. Love of all the world's peoples does not exclude love of one's country. The advantage of the part in a world society is best served by promoting the advantage of the whole. Current international activities in various fields which nurture mutual affection and a sense of solidarity among peoples need greatly to be increased.

Religious strife, throughout history, has been the cause of innumerable wars and conflicts, a major blight to progress, and is increasingly abhorrent to the people of all faiths and no faith. Followers of all religions must be willing to face the basic questions which this strife raises, and to arrive at clear answers. How are the differences between them to be resolved, both in theory and in practice? The challenge facing the religious leaders of mankind is to contemplate, with hearts filled with the spirit of compassion and a desire for truth, the plight of humanity, and to ask themselves whether they cannot, in humility before their Almighty Creator, submerge their theological differences in a great spirit of mutual forbearance that will enable them to work together for the advancement of human understanding and peace.

The emancipation of women, the achievement of full equality between the sexes, is one of the most important, though less acknowledged prerequisites of peace. The denial of such equality perpetrates an injustice against one half of the world's population and promotes in men harmful attitudes and habits that are carried from the family to the workplace, to political life, and ultimately to international relations. There are no grounds, moral, practical, or biological, upon which such denial can be justified. Only as women are welcomed into full partnership in all fields of human endeavour will the moral and psychological climate be created in which international peace can emerge.

The cause of universal education, which has already enlisted in its service an army of dedicated people from every faith and nation, deserves the utmost support that the governments of the world can lend it. For ignorance is indisputably the principal reason for the decline and fall of peoples and the perpetuation of prejudice. No nation can achieve success unless education is accorded all its citizens. Lack of resources limits the ability of many nations to fulfil this necessity, imposing a certain ordering of priorities. The decision-making agencies involved would do well to consider giving first priority to the education of women and girls, since it is through educated mothers that the benefits of knowledge can be most effectively and rapidly diffused throughout society. In keeping with the requirements of the times, consideration should also be given to teaching the concept of world citizenship as part of the standard education of every child.

A fundamental lack of communication between peoples seriously undermines efforts towards world peace. Adopting an international auxiliary language would go far to resolving this problem and necessitates the most urgent attention.

Two points bear emphasizing in all these issues. One is that the abolition of war is not simply a matter of signing treaties and protocols; it is a complex task requiring a new level of commitment to resolving issues not customarily associated with the pursuit of peace. Based on political agreements alone, the idea of collective security is a chimera. The other point is that the primary challenge in dealing with issues of peace is to raise the context to the level of principle, as distinct from pure pragmatism. For, in essence, peace stems from an inner state supported by a spiritual or moral attitude, and it is chiefly in evoking this attitude that the possibility of enduring solutions can be found.

There are spiritual principles, or what some call human values, by which solutions can be found for every social problem. Any well-intentioned group can in a general sense devise practical solutions to its problems, but good intentions and practical knowledge are usually not enough. The essential merit of spiritual principle is that it not only presents a perspective which harmonizes with that which is immanent in human nature, it also induces an attitude, a dynamic, a will, an aspiration, which facilitate the discovery and implementation of practical measures. Leaders of governments and all in authority would be well served in their efforts to solve problems if they would first seek to identify the principles involved and then be guided by them.

III

The primary question to be resolved is how the present world, with its entrenched pattern of conflict, can change to a world in which harmony and co-operation will prevail.

World order can be founded only on an unshakeable consciousness of the oneness of mankind, a spiritual truth which all the human sciences confirm. Anthropology, physiology, psychology, recognize only one human species, albeit infinitely varied in the secondary aspects of life. Recognition of this truth requires abandonment of prejudice—prejudice of every kind—race, class, colour, creed, nation, sex, degree of material civilization, everything which enables people to consider themselves superior to others.

Acceptance of the oneness of mankind is the first fundamental prerequisite for reorganization and administration of the world as one country, the home of humankind. Universal acceptance of this spiritual principle is essential to any successful attempt to establish world peace. It should therefore be universally proclaimed, taught in schools, and constantly asserted in every nation as preparation for the organic change in the structure of society which it implies.

In the Bahá'í view, recognition of the oneness of mankind "calls for no less than the reconstruction and the demilitarization of the whole civilized world—a world organically unified in all the essential aspects of its life, its political machinery, its spiritual aspiration, its trade and finance, its script and language, and yet infinite in the diversity of the national characteristics of its federated units."

Elaborating the implications of this pivotal principle, Shoghi Effendi, the Guardian of the Bahá'í Faith, commented in 1931 that: "Far from aiming at the subversion of the existing foundations of society, it seeks to broaden its basis, to remold its institutions in a manner consonant with the needs of an ever-changing world. It can conflict with no legitimate allegiances, nor can it undermine essential loyalties. Its purpose is neither to stifle the flame of a sane and intelligent patriotism in men's hearts, nor to abolish the system of national autonomy so essential if the evils of excessive centralization are to be avoided. It does not ignore, nor does it attempt to suppress, the diversity of ethnical origins, of climate, of history, of language and tradition, of thought and habit, that differentiate the peoples and nations of the world. It calls for a wider loyalty, for a larger aspiration than any that has animated the human race. It insists upon the subordination of national impulses and interests to the imperative claims of a unified world. It repudiates excessive centralization on one hand, and disclaims all attempts at uniformity on the other. Its watchword is unity in diversity..."

The achievement of such ends requires several stages in the adjustment of national political attitudes, which now verge on anarchy in the absence of clearly defined laws or universally accepted and enforceable principles regulating the relationships between nations. The League of Nations, the United Nations, and the many organizations and agreements produced by them have unquestionably been helpful in attenuating some of the negative effects of international conflicts, but they have shown themselves incapable of preventing war. Indeed, there have been scores of wars since the end of the Second World War; many are yet raging.

The predominant aspects of this problem had already emerged in the nineteenth century when Bahá'u'lláh first advanced his proposals for the establishment of world peace. The principle of collective security was propounded by him in statements addressed to the rulers of the world. Shoghi Effendi commented on his meaning: "What else could these weighty words signify," he wrote, "if they did not point to the inevitable curtailment of unfettered national sovereignty as an indispensable preliminary to the formation of the future Commonwealth of all the nations of the world? Some form of a world super-state must needs be evolved, in whose favour all the nations of the world will have willingly ceded every claim to make war, certain rights to impose taxation and all rights to maintain armaments, except for purposes of maintaining internal order within their respective dominions. Such a state will have to include within its orbit an International Executive adequate to enforce supreme and unchallengeable authority on every recalcitrant member of the commonwealth; a World Parliament whose members shall be elected by the people in their respective countries and whose election shall be confirmed by their respective governments; and a Supreme Tribunal whose judgement will have a binding effect even in such cases where the parties concerned did not voluntarily agree to submit their case to its consideration.

"A world community in which all economic barriers will have been permanently demolished and the interdependence of capital and labour definitely recognized; in which the clamour of religious fanaticism and strife will have been forever stilled; in which the flame of racial animosity will have been finally extinguished; in which a single code of international law—the product of the considered judgement of the world's federated representatives—shall have as its sanction the instant and coercive intervention of the combined forces of the federated units; and finally a world community in which the fury of a capricious and militant nationalism will have been transmuted into an abiding consciousness of world citizenship—such indeed, appears, in its broadest outline, the Order anticipated by Bahá'u'lláh, an Order that shall come to be regarded as the fairest fruit of a slowly maturing age."

The implementation of these far-reaching measures was indicated by Bahá'u'lláh: "The time must come when the imperative necessity for the holding of a vast, an all-embracing assemblage of men will be universally realized. The rulers and kings of the earth must needs attend it, and, participating in its deliberations, must consider such ways and means as will lay the foundations of the world's Great Peace amongst men."

The courage, the resolution, the pure motive, the selfless love of one people for another—all the spiritual and moral qualities required for effecting this momentous step towards peace are focused on the will to act. And it is towards arousing the necessary volition that earnest consideration must be given to the reality of man, namely, his thought. To understand the relevance of this potent reality is also to appreciate the social necessity of actualizing its unique value through candid, dispassionate and cordial consultation, and of acting upon the results of this process. Bahá'u'lláh insistently drew attention to the virtues and indispensability of consultation for ordering human affairs. He said: "Consultation bestows greater awareness and transmutes conjecture into certitude. It is a shining light which, in a dark world, leads the way and guides. For everything there is and will continue to be a station of perfection and maturity. The maturity of the gift of understanding is made manifest through consultation." The very attempt to achieve peace through the consultative action he proposed can release such a salutary spirit among the peoples of the earth that no power could resist the final, triumphal outcome.

Concerning the proceedings for this world gathering, 'Abdu'l-Bahá, the son of Bahá'u'lláh and authorized interpreter of his teachings, offered these insights: "They must make the Cause of Peace the object of general consultation, and seek by every means in their power to establish a Union of the nations of the world. They must conclude a binding treaty and establish a covenant, the provisions of which shall be sound, inviolable and definite. They must proclaim it to all the world and obtain for it the sanction of all the human race. This supreme and noble undertaking—the real source of the peace and well-being of all the world—should be regarded as sacred by all that dwell on earth. All the forces of humanity must be mobilized to ensure the stability and permanence of this Most Great Covenant. In this all-embracing Pact the limits and frontiers of each and every nation should be clearly fixed, the principles underlying the relations of governments towards one another definitely laid down, and all international agreements and obligations ascertained. In like manner, the size of the armaments of every government should be strictly limited, for if the preparations for war and the military forces of any nation should be allowed to increase, they will arouse the suspicion of others. The fundamental principle underlying this solemn Pact should be so fixed that if any government later violate any one of its provisions, all the governments on earth should arise to reduce it to utter submission, nay the human race as a whole should resolve, with every power at its disposal, to destroy that government. Should this greatest of all remedies be applied to the sick body of the world, it will assuredly recover from its ills and will remain eternally safe and secure."

The holding of this mighty convocation is long overdue.

With all the ardour of our hearts, we appeal to the leaders of all nations to seize this opportune moment and take irreversible steps to convoke this world meeting. All the forces of history impel the human race towards this act which will mark for all time the dawn of its long-awaited maturity.

Will not the United Nations, with the full support of its membership, rise to the high purposes of such a crowning event?

Let men and women, youth and children everywhere recognize the eternal merit of this imperative action for all peoples and lift up their voices in willing assent. Indeed, let it be this generation that inaugurates this glorious stage in the evolution of social life on the planet.

IV

The source of the optimism we feel is a vision transcending the cessation of war and the creation of agencies of international co-operation. Permanent peace among nations is an essential stage, but not, Bahá'u'lláh asserts, the ultimate goal of the social development of humanity. Beyond the initial armistice forced upon the world by the fear of nuclear holocaust, beyond the political peace reluctantly entered into by suspicious rival nations, beyond pragmatic arrangements for security and coexistence, beyond even the many experiments in co-operation which these steps will make possible lies the crowning goal: the unification of all the peoples of the world in one universal family.

Disunity is a danger that the nations and peoples of the earth can no longer endure; the consequences are too terrible to contemplate, too obvious to require any demonstration. "The well-being of mankind," Bahá'u'lláh wrote more than a century ago, "its peace and security, are unattainable unless and until its unity is firmly established." In observing that "mankind is groaning, is dying to be led to unity, and to terminate its age-long martyrdom," Shoghi Effendi further commented that: "Unification of the whole of mankind is the hall-mark of the stage which human society is now approaching. Unity of family, of tribe, of city-state, and nation have been successively attempted and fully established. World unity is the goal towards which a harassed humanity is striving. Nation-building has come to an end. The anarchy inherent in state sovereignty is moving towards a climax. A world, growing to maturity, must abandon this fetish, recognize the oneness and wholeness of human relationships, and establish once for all the machinery that can best incarnate this fundamental principle of its life."

All contemporary forces of change validate this view. The proofs can be discerned in the many examples already cited of the favourable signs towards world peace in current international movements and developments. The army of men and women, drawn from virtually every culture, race and nation on earth, who serve the multifarious agencies of the United Nations, represent a planetary "civil service" whose impressive accomplishments are indicative of the degree of co-operation that can be attained even under discouraging conditions. An urge towards unity, like a spiritual springtime, struggles to express itself through countless international congresses that bring together people from a vast array of disciplines. It motivates appeals for international projects involving children and youth. Indeed, it is the real source of the remarkable movement towards ecumenism by which members of historically antagonistic religions and sects seem irresistibly drawn towards one another. Together with the opposing tendency to warfare and self-aggrandizement against which it ceaselessly struggles, the drive towards world unity is one of the dominant, pervasive features of life on the planet during the closing years of the twentieth century.

The experience of the Bahá'í community may be seen as an example of this enlarging unity. It is a community of some three to four million people drawn from many nations, cultures, classes and creeds, engaged in a wide range of activities serving the spiritual, social and economic needs of the peoples of many lands. It is a single social organism, representative of the diversity of the human family, conducting its affairs through a system of commonly accepted consultative principles, and cherishing equally all the great outpourings of divine guidance in human history. Its existence is yet another convincing proof of the practicality of its Founder's vision of a united world, another evidence that humanity can live as one global society, equal to whatever challenges its coming of age may entail. If the Bahá'í experience can contribute in whatever measure to reinforcing hope in the unity of the human race, we are happy to offer it as a model for study.

In contemplating the supreme importance of the task now challenging the entire world, we bow our heads in humility before the awesome majesty of the divine Creator, Who out of His infinite love has created all humanity from the same stock; exalted the gem-like reality of man; honoured it with intellect and wisdom, nobility and immortality; and conferred upon man the "unique distinction and capacity to know Him and to love Him," a capacity that "must needs be regarded as the generating impulse and the primary purpose underlying the whole of creation."

We hold firmly the conviction that all human beings have been created "to carry forward an ever-advancing civilization;" that "to act like the beasts of the field is unworthy of man;" that the virtues that befit human dignity are trustworthiness, forbearance, mercy, compassion and loving-kindness towards all peoples. We reaffirm the belief that the "potentialities inherent in the station of man, the full measure of his destiny on earth, the innate excellence of his reality, must all be manifested in this promised Day of God." These are the motivations for our unshakeable faith that unity and peace are the attainable goal towards which humanity is striving.

At this writing, the expectant voices of Bahá'ís can be heard despite the persecution they still endure in the land in which their Faith was born. By their example of steadfast hope, they bear witness to the belief that the imminent realization of this age-old dream of peace is now, by virtue of the transforming effects of Bahá'u'lláh's revelation, invested with the force of divine authority. Thus we convey to you not only a vision in words: we summon the power of deeds of faith and sacrifice; we convey the anxious plea of our co-religionists everywhere for peace and unity. We join with all who are the victims of aggression, all who yearn for an end to conflict and contention, all whose devotion to principles of peace and world order promotes the ennobling purposes for which humanity was called into being by an all-loving Creator.

In the earnestness of our desire to impart to you the fervour of our hope and the depth of our confidence, we cite the emphatic promise of Bahá'u'lláh: "These fruitless strifes, these ruinous wars shall pass away, and the 'Most Great Peace' shall come."

APPENDIX 3

SUPPORTING THE BAHÁ'Í CHAIR FOR WORLD PEACE

To support its many and diverse operations, the Bahá'í Chair depends largely on contributions it receives thanks to the generosity of donors. For information about the Chair, please see pages ix-xi or visit www.bahaichair.umd.edu.

The Bahá'í Chair for World Peace at the University of Maryland welcomes your support in raising awareness about its important and timely mission in examining pathways to peace. As a self-supporting academic program, the Bahá'í Chair for World Peace is grateful for and appreciates contributions of any amount in support of its activities.

If you would like to consider making a financial gift, there are two funds to which you can contribute:

1. CONTRIBUTE TO THE OPERATIONS ACCOUNT

    Contributing to the operations of the Chair makes its numerous and varied programmatic activities possible. Those who wish to contribute to the operations account should make checks payable to:

    USMF, Inc.
    Memo: **Bahá'í Chair Operations***

2. GIVE TO THE ENDOWMENT

    For its basic operation, the Chair depends on an endowment fund from which it receives its annual budget. Those who wish to contribute to the endowment should make checks payable to:

    USMF, Inc.
    Memo: **Bahá'í Chair Endowment***

* To ensure that your donation reaches the account you choose with the least difficulty, it is important that your check be made payable exactly as stated above. Thank you for your help and generosity.

(Please see the following page for mailing address.)

KINDLY SEND DONATIONS TO:

The Bahá'í Chair for World Peace
Dr. Hoda Mahmoudi
1114 Chincoteague Hall
University of Maryland
College Park, MD 20742

A letter of thanks and confirmation will be sent upon receipt of your contribution.

Made in the USA
Charleston, SC
07 August 2014